Business and Higher Education: Toward New Alliances

Gerard G. Gold, *Editor*

NEW DIRECTIONS FOR EXPERIENTIAL LEARNING

Sponsored by the Council for the Advancement of Experiential Learning (CAEL)

PAMELA J. TATE, *Editor-in-Chief*;
MORRIS T. KEETON, *Consulting Editor*

Number 13, September 1981

Paperback sourcebooks in
The Jossey-Bass Higher Education Series

Jossey-Bass Inc., Publishers
San Francisco • Washington • London

Business and Higher Education: Toward New Alliances
Number 13, September 1981
Gerard G. Gold, *Editor*

New Directions for Experiential Learning Series
Pamela J. Tate, *Editor-in-Chief*
Morris T. Keeton, *Consulting Editor*

New Directions for Experiential Learning is published quarterly
by Jossey-Bass Inc., Publishers, and is sponsored by the Council
for the Advancement of Experiential Learning (CAEL).

Correspondence:
Subscriptions, single-issue orders, change of address notices,
undelivered copies, and other correspondence should be sent to
New Directions Subscriptions, Jossey-Bass Inc., Publishers,
433 California Street, San Francisco, California 94104.

Editorial correspondence should be sent to the Editor-in-Chief,
Pamela J. Tate or the Consulting Editor, Morris T. Keeton
at the Council for the Advancement of Experiential Learning (CAEL),
Suite 300, Lakefront North, Columbia, Maryland 21044.

Library of Congress Catalogue Card Number LC 80-84277

International Standard Serial Number ISSN 0271-0595

International Standard Book Number ISBN 87589-828-9

Cover art by Willi Baum

Manufactured in the United States of America

Ordering Information

The paperback sourcebooks listed below are published quarterly and can be ordered either by subscription or single-copy.

Subscriptions cost $30.00 per year for institutions, agencies, and libraries. Individuals can subscribe at the special rate of $18.00 per year *if payment is by personal check.* (Note that the full rate of $30.00 applies if payment is by institutional check, even if the subscription is designated for an individual.) Standing orders are accepted.

Single copies are available at $6.95 when payment accompanies order, and *all single-copy orders under $25.00 must include payment.* (California, Washington, D.C., New Jersey, and New York residents please include appropriate sales tax.) For billed orders, cost per copy is $6.95 plus postage and handling. (Prices subject to change without notice.)

To ensure correct and prompt delivery, all orders must give either the *name of an individual* or an *official purchase order number.* Please submit your order as follows:

Subscriptions: specify series and subscription year.
Single Copies: specify sourcebook code and issue number (such as, IR8).

Mail orders for United States and Possessions, Latin America, Canada, Japan, Australia, and New Zealand to:
  Jossey-Bass Inc., Publishers
  433 California Street
  San Francisco, California 94104

Mail orders for all other parts of the world to:
  Jossey-Bass Limited
  28 Banner Street
  London EC1Y 8QE

New Directions for Experiential Learning Series
Pamela J. Tate, *Editor-in-Chief*
Morris T. Keeton, *Consulting Editor*

EL1 *Learning by Experience—What, Why, How,* Morris T. Keeton, Pamela J. Tate
EL2 *Developing and Expanding Cooperative Education,* James W. Wilson
EL3 *Defining and Measuring Competence,* Paul S. Pottinger, Joan Goldsmith
EL4 *Transferring Experiential Credit,* S. V. Martorana, Eileen Kuhns
EL5 *Combining Career Development with Experiential Learning,* Frank D. van Aalst
EL6 *Enriching the Liberal Arts Through Experiential Learning,* Stevens Brooks, James Althof
EL7 *Developing New Adult Clienteles by Recognizing Prior Learning,* Rexford G. Moon, Gene R. Hawes
EL8 *Developing Experiential Learning Programs for Professional Education,* Eugene T. Byrne, Douglas E. Wolfe

Publications Available from CAEL

Assessing Occupational Competences — A CAEL Handbook, Amiel Sharon
College-Sponsored Experiential Learning — A CAEL Handbook, John Duley and Sheila Gordon
College-Sponsored Experiential Learning — A CAEL Student Guide, Hadley and Nesbitt
"Developing and Expanding Cooperative Education," *New Directions for Experiential
  Learning,* number 2, Pamela J. Tate and Morris T. Keeton, Editors
Efficient Evaluation of Individual Performance in Field Placement, Stephen L. Yelon and
  John S. Duley
Lifelong Learning: Purposes and Priorities, K. Patricia Cross

Contents

Preface

Probably the most used phrase in prefaces—and the least accurate—is "this book breaks new ground." However, this sourcebook really does. For the first time, a reader can find in one volume a theoretical framework for interpreting programs and issues in collaboration, an excellent history of how we have developed alliances between higher education and business over the last 100 years, a representative description of the alliances that now exist, the results of a federal agency's efforts to make higher education more open to new kinds of interactions with business, and a model for economic development partnerships at the local level. As one who recommended in 1977 that higher education should begin developing and studying new alliances with industry, I believe this book represents an important overview of what is possible.

Several things can now be said with confidence about the development of these alliances. There is a "second system" of postsecondary education located in industry, representing an investment level of $30 billion to $50 billion. Its size and value are coming close to the net worth of the 3,500 colleges and universities, whose total investment is about $55 billion. The range of instruction in this second system is as wide as in colleges and universities—from maintenance of photocopiers to basic research and theory in polymer chemistry. Furthermore, there is no good evidence that any form of instruction and content "belongs" only in one sector and not in the other.

We are developing a critical mass of alliances between industry and higher education, many of which are creative and mutually satisfactory. Those alliances involve teaching courses, offering degrees, trading goods, services and people, combining resources, doing research. In the larger view, the efforts are part of a push to increase the sense of self-fulfillment and control over one's life that are characteristic of the human resource development movement in industry, the faculty development movement, and the "self-directed learning" movement in higher education. The changing occupational structure will demand increased levels of education in the future as well.

However, some questions remain: How should these relationships be coordinated and by whom? What will be the role of various governmental agencies in regulating the "quality" of voluntary coordination? Who should prepare teachers for education programs in industry? What will become of the liberal arts in all of this? (My thesis on that one is that the work force will age rapidly from 1985 to 2000 and that liberal arts for workers over forty will be very popular.) What will be the role of these new alliances in educational policy, especially at state and federal levels?

Although the system of noncollegiate postsecondary education has unquestionably expanded in recent years, our knowledge of the system has increased even more rapidly. As our awareness of the "learning system" increases in the future, we may discern new patterns that will not only illuminate new tasks for each of the two systems, and for the interactions between them, but we may also discover new routes of access to both systems for a variety of people, increasing the quality of many lives and enriching the resources of our society.

Harold L. Hodgkinson
NTL Institute

Harold L. Hodgkinson is president of NTL Institute in Arlington, Virginia. Previously he was executive director of the Professional Institute of the American Management Associations and director of the National Institute of Education.

Editor's Notes

This sourcebook examines higher education–business relations as they exist at present, as they are changing, and as they could be in the next decade if different strategies are pursued by leaders in both sectors. Underlying our discussions of institutional relationships, however, is a more fundamental concern: Who and where is the individual learner in all of the changes?

Although this book emphasizes the interests of the higher education and business sectors, some attention to the roles of labor organizations and government is inevitable and useful. The structure and content of business–higher education relationships in America can only be understood in a context that includes these other sets of institutional relations. Readers are referred to a companion volume in this series: *Building New Alliances: Labor Unions and Higher Education* (Stack and Hutton, 1980).

Learning can occur at any time, in any place. The attempts of higher education and business to assume some larger degree of responsibility for the quality and content of individual learning in nontraditional settings can be seen as either assistance to or as intrusion on the efforts of individuals to find their ways in the world. Individuals are intimately affected by the ways in which higher education and business carry out their respective responsibilities.

Colleges and corporations alike endorse, and even claim to provide sanctuary to, the concept of individualism. Likewise, both claim major contributions to the aggregate mental energy and wealth of the nation. Free-market capitalism, academic freedom, and the core sociopolitical freedoms of speech and religion are each different but essential pillars of American values and institutions (Stauffer, 1980).

Yet a key distinction is that while the aim of business is to direct individualism toward the production of economic wealth, the core aim of education is to direct individualism toward self-knowledge and from that self-knowledge toward world knowledge, of which economic wealth is but one part. If there is a corporation where Kant, calculus, Marxian economics, anthropology, engineering, basket-weaving, and yoga are taught, it is an exception to the rule, and probably a marvel. Under the aegis of higher education such a melange is merely to be expected. However, few would rely on a higher education institution to successfully launch a space shuttle, produce and market a new soap, or manufacture computers on a large scale. This distinction creates strains that inevitably are felt in the formation of serious relationships and alliances between higher education and business.

Questions of the actual (rather than theoretical) impact of corporate control over educational resources have hardly been broached at this early stage of a much-encouraged relationship. Despite a history of both consensus and dissonance, present corporate-education relationships are seen largely as a benign counterbalance to government influence and regulation (Council for Financial Aid to Education, 1977).

Mindful that the history of these relationships has been both complex and at times emotional, Gold argues in the first chapter that today's corporate and university educators are probably witnesses to, and often participants in, a historic shift in the nature of the basic relationship. Undergirding this shift is the concept of lifelong learning, which recognizes the need for a variety of providers of education and training services in addition to traditional higher education institutions, as well as the fact that educational purposes and methods are becoming more central to the effectiveness of all social organizations. These developments have been long-awaited by proponents of a "learning society" but may not carry with them the prestige and enrollment benefits frequently anticipated for colleges and universities. The die has not been cast on what the structure of the future adult education system will be. Communications, leadership, and programs that move beyond campus and corporate confines are critically needed at the local, state, and national levels. Gold argues that postsecondary educators will need to demonstrate that the quality of their institutional performance justifies their case for more corporate, governmental, and public support and financing.

Craig and Evers portray the world of corporate education and training. Summarizing the 100-year history of employer-initiated education and training programs, they demonstrate that the "shadow education system" is coming to claim its rightful place as a major component of a larger adult learning system. They point out that the dramatic growth of this system during the last decade reflects the increasing importance of training to corporate planning and development. As this function increases in importance, the desire of management to exercise close control over the content, staffing, scheduling, and costs of training also increases. Similarly, the importance of training also increases the visibility of training directors and staff within their organizations. Craig and Evers make a strong case for collaboration based on more open communications and greater use of a needs assessment approach to corporate-campus program development.

Johnson and Tornatzky examine university and industry roles in creating technological change and generally improving the process of technological innovation. Focusing on "boundary-spanning" mechanisms and the incentives and disincentives for collaborative research projects involving the two sectors, they reveal numerous policy questions that come to the fore when popularly held assumptions about university-based research are questioned. For example, it is far from likely that a linear relationship exists between basic research and economically viable product development, that universities are the optimum place to perform basic research, or that universities are in fact capable of providing trained scientific and engineering personnel in response to labor market demands (National Science Foundation and the Department of Education, 1980). Given that the federal government supports about 70 percent of the nation's $7 billion basic research expenditures, that universities and colleges perform more than one-half of the nation's basic research, that more than two-thirds of higher education–based research and development is paid for by direct federal support, and that national policy appears to be shifting toward encouragement of industry-university cooperative research, this discussion is of critical importance (Office of Management and Budget, 1981).

Lynton's chapter raises an almost subliminal issue. He finds in the comparison of corporate training and higher education a difference in ethos: a pervasive emphasis on tasks, interpersonal relationships, and teamwork in the former and an equally pervasive emphasis on cognition and discretely individualistic learning in the latter. Off the sports field, few colleges have a curriculum that requires teamwork. The shock of employment is frequently a cultural shock in adjusting to a new motivational system built on the interdependencies among colleagues. Another key concern he expresses is the difference between systems of access to education. Education and training in industry frequently is a reward for individuals selected for promotion. Consequently, the most important decisions about who learns are in the hands of supervisors, in sharp contrast to the present, almost open-ended structure of higher education with its dependence on learner-based decisions. Lynton perceives the possibility that the corporate training profession may isolate itself with its own jargon, in-bred promotion networks, and fixed ideas on how to teach. His call for greater communication between the two sectors is a call to reinforce the creative talents of both sectors.

DeMeester brings the perspective of the Fund for the Improvement of Postsecondary Education. FIPSE's impact on innovative practices in American colleges, universities, and noncollegiate adult learning agencies has been profound. Making innovation respectable, giving local initiatives national recognition, building networks of effective practitioners, and nurturing adult learner policy issues through debate and demonstration have been salient characteristics of FIPSE's "seed money," foundation grants approach to institutional change. As DeMeester points out, failing to ask what is the benefit of a proposed activity to the learner can undermine the credibility and effectiveness of interinstitutional projects. Starting from the learner's needs requires clarity about the diversity of individual and institutional resources available within a community, skill in designing programs that make effective use of those resources, and reliability and flexibility in human relations and administration. Future success in higher education–corporate relations—whether at national, state, or local, chief executive or action officer levels—will be built upon the trust and satisfaction that grows out of proven performance, reliability, honesty, and resourcefulness in thousands of projects and personal experiences.

Academic credit for learning from work and life experience took firm hold during the 1970s as a valid and useful concept (Keeton and Tate, 1978). Its validity was rooted in common sense and education theory: Learning takes place in all walks of life with or without direct supervision of an authorized instructor. Controversy still surrounds the concept because assessing and validating learner competence, knowledge gained through experience, and noncampus courses requires evaluation methods that hardly existed early in the decade. Also, some saw the acceptance of self-directed or off-campus learning as a threat to the raison d'etre of formal institutions of learning (Pottinger and Goldsmith, 1979). But higher educators were also intrigued by the thought that greater flexibility in working with and credentialing independent learners would open avenues to more adult enrollments.

As the chapter by Reilly and McGarraghy makes clear, there is some truth in each case. Academic credit and credentialing by academic institutions are highly valued by many adult learners and are viewed by many employers as signs of quality control and achievement. The tools developed by educational reformers in the past decade are now being used to validate formal instruction and self-directed study for which the campus acts primarily as certifier and record keeper. Though increasingly supportive, faculty remain unclear as to the full impact of such ventures as the New York Program on Noncollegiate Sponsored Instruction. On the one hand, the amount of direct instruction by college faculty within a given degree program may decrease, along with full-time enrollments and the use of certain campus facilities. On the other hand, the value of higher education institutions to their communities may be enhanced, and colleges may be able to use the "bait" of off-campus experience and instruction to reach the wider audiences of high school graduates, college dropouts, and working adults who would not previously have considered the wider academic curriculum that employers are not equipped to offer.

Kyle proposes one interinstitutional idea for the future, the concept of a human resources management center (HRMC). The HRMC would be a community-based organization for monitoring and managing economic factors causing structural and cyclical imbalances in local labor markets. Kyle argues that only at the local labor market level can pragmatic, organization-sensitive leadership put in place the intricate structure of communications, needs assessment, analysis, and technical assistance needed to solve the real problems of real people in real organizations on a sustained, year-to-year basis. Many pieces of the HRMC concept are already in place, largely unnoticed and unused by their own communities. Kyle suggests that the potential of the concept will only be realized if national corporate, union, government, and education leaders take responsibility for its advocacy and demonstration funding. The key points of her chapter reflect the overall perspective of this volume: that national problems must be tackled effectively at the local level, that multisector collaboration is required to solve those problems, and that the leadership skills and techniques for implementing local collaborative action are available but need concerted development and advocacy.

It is our hope that each of the chapters will provide examples of and insight into strategies for more effective relationships, even alliances, between higher education and business institutions. We are not talking in this sourcebook about a single institution's own strategy for survival or growth. For assistance in developing such a strategy, postsecondary educators should consult publications such as *Three Thousand Futures: The Next 20 Years for Higher Education* (Carnegie Council on Policy Studies in Higher Education, 1980), the work of the National Center for Higher Education Management Systems in Boulder, Colorado, and the National Institute of Education's *Higher Education Planning: A Bibliographic Handbook* (Halstead, 1979). Nor are we talking about the counterpart literature of corporate strategic planning such as is found in Schendel and Hofer's *Strategic Management: A New View of Business Policy and Planning* (1979).

Instead, we have tried to include strategies for developing creative and balanced relationships between higher education and business institutions. Far from sketching out comprehensive models and plans, we believe that effective strategies evolve from effective leadership and clear communication, and that creative opportunism can be rooted in a clear assessment of institutional missions that sets the standards for decisions.

Gerard G. Gold
Editor

References

Carnegie Council on Policy Studies in Higher Education. *Three Thousand Futures: The Next Twenty Years for Higher Education.* San Francisco: Jossey-Bass, 1980.

Council for Financial Aid to Education. *The Corporate Stake in Higher Education.* New York: Council for Financial Aid to Education, 1977.

Halstead, D. K. (Ed.). *Higher Education Planning: A Bibliographic Handbook.* Washington, D.C.: National Institute of Education, 1979.

Keeton, M. T., and Tate, P. J. (Eds.). *New Directions for Experiential Learning:*

8

Learning by Experience—What, Why, How, no. 1. San Francisco: Jossey-Bass, 1978.

National Science Foundation and U.S. Department of Education. *Science and Engineering Education for the 1980s and Beyond.* Washington, D.C.: National Science Foundation and U.S. Department of Education, 1980.

Office of Management and Budget. *Special Analysis K: Research and Development.* Washington, D.C.: Office of Management and Budget, January 1981.

Pottinger, P. S., and Goldsmith, J. (Eds.). *New Directions for Experiential Learning: Defining and Measuring Competence,* no. 3. San Francisco: Jossey-Bass, 1979.

Schendel, D. E., and Hofer, C. W. *Strategic Management: A New View of Business Policy and Planning.* Boston: Little Brown, 1979.

Stack, H., and Hutton, C. M. (Eds.). *New Directions for Experiential Learning: Building New Alliances: Labor Unions and Higher Education,* no. 10. San Francisco: Jossey-Bass, 1980.

Stauffer, T. M. (Ed.). *Agenda for Business and Higher Education.* Washington, D.C.: American Council on Education, 1980.

Gerard G. Gold is a senior program officer at the National Institute for Work and Learning, a private, nonprofit organization concerned with the development and implementation of education-work policies and practices. He directs the Institute's Industry-Education-Labor Collaboration Project for the U.S. Department of Education.

Business–higher education relationships have been built around teaching/learning, new ideas and products, flow of human resources, and strategy development. As education and employment institutions become major components of a lifelong learning system, new strategies and mechanisms for communication are needed.

Toward Business–Higher Education Alliances

Gerard G. Gold

As we become more of a learning society, it becomes progressively more difficult to decide where the university ends and the corporate world begins and where they both fit within the larger education and training system, which includes unions, public-sector agencies, professional associations, libraries, parks, cable television and other media publishers, educational brokers, alternative education organizations, and other local providers and consumers. The very boundaries of a university or college seem to disappear when corporations grant degrees, when colleges engage in more technical training, and when learners increasingly receive college credit for learning through life and work experiences outside the academy. It is not at all clear whether the blurring of these boundaries ought to be taken as a welcome opportunity or an emerging problem.

Because what we do on the "boundaries" of our society—how wide we set those boundaries and how inclusively we define tolerable behavior—tells us how free we truly are as a nation, the academic sanctuary is important. In other words, the academy's alliances with the real world are

The work upon which this article is based was performed pursuant to Contract #300790691 with the Office of Vocational and Adult Education of the U.S. Department of Education.

G. Gold (Ed.), *New Directions for Experiential Learning: Business and Higher Education—Towards New Alliances*, no. 13. San Francisco: Jossey-Bass, September 1981.

9

still limited by its essential function of protecting inquiry and criticism in all disciplines—whether in matters scientific, political, aesthetic, or economic. And it is still the case that the freedom of belief and speech, the freedom to be critical, is more frequently, albeit not perfectly, protected in university than in corporate settings. It is therefore important to ask to what extent any proposed or operating linkage between the business and higher education communities may restrict or expand either institution's ability to define and enforce its own sense of proper behavior. That these boundaries and restrictions exist is readily acknowledged providing a source of endlessly ebbing and flowing debate (Ravitch, 1978; Feinberg and others, 1980). Whether the present enthusiasm for postsecondary liaisons with the corporate community may be of such a scale as to force historic shifts in the relationship is a more immediate and substantial question.

The question is made even more complex by the fact that postsecondary institutions, having become increasingly dependent on federal and state government aid, are now battered by government regulations and declining enrollments among youth (Giamatti, 1980; Moynihan, 1980). In the face of declining resources, institutions are turning toward corporations in search of sympathy, political allies, and new resources and enrollments—perhaps without thinking through the consequences of these alliances.

After briefly reviewing the history of relationships between business and higher education, this chapter will discuss the present setting for such alliances from the perspective of the four basic functions that characterize business–higher education collaboration: (1) the production and distribution of teaching/learning services; (2) the production and distribution of new ideas and products; (3) the flow of human resources between education and employment; and (4) the process of strategy development for higher education–business relationships. Issues and strategies for the future will then be presented.

History of Higher Education–Business Relationships

From about a century ago, when the creation of Johns Hopkins and Cornell signaled the active involvement of industrialists in formulating the new purposes, content and methods of higher education, the two worlds have been interlocked. Thorstein Veblen, for example, observed eighty years ago that it was the inexorable influence of the modern corporation and its industries that first moved the established higher education institutions away from classical studies and toward research (Veblen, [1899] 1953).

According to Veysey (1965), the 1890s marked the first time that overt student recruitment strategies were employed. College presidents and professors catered to a wider clientele: "Bearing such titles as 'The Practical Value of a College Education,' 'Does College Education Pay?' and 'College

Men First Among Successful Citizens,' these writings helped establish an atmosphere of welcome for boys of worldly aspiration" (p. 348). This period initiated the credentialing function of higher education and "old boy networks" that have become such core elements of the higher education–business human resource system. Thus began the first great wave of democratization in American higher education, with the new corporate management class most in mind.

The founders of Johns Hopkins, Cornell, the land grant state universities, and the early technical colleges were enthusiastic about the contributions of American industry to the wealth—both intellectual and economic—of the nation and to its position in world affairs. They welcomed the concept of stewardship, that wealth was entrusted by God into the hands of capable individuals whose personal responsibility it was to distribute that wealth to benefit the society at large. More than welcomed, philanthropy was expected from the private sector (Veysey, 1965).

Not all were persuaded by this argument, however. On the one hand, many fortunes never found their way to public purpose despite the examples of Rockefeller, Carnegie, and others. On the other hand, numerous scholars resisted too close an association with "monied interests: "

No academic trend excited more heated comment at the time than this one. John Dewey asserted in 1902: 'Institutions (of learning) are ranked by their obvious material prosperity, until the atmosphere of money-getting and money-spending hides from view the interests for the sake of which money alone has a place.' In an extreme form such indictments charged that university leaders took their orders, more or less directly, from industrial magnates. Harvard's John Jay Chapman noted that 'as the boss has been the tool of businessmen in politics, so the college president has been his agent in education' " (Veysey, 1965, p. 346).

This pattern of attraction and avoidance continues today. Corporate philanthropic support for education, $870 million in 1979, has averaged about 36 percent of all corporate giving annually for the last fifteen years (Council for Financial Aid to Education, n.d.). But corporate interest is not without reservations. While 96 percent of 292 corporate chief executives surveyed in 1979 agreed that "corporate self-interest is best served by preserving the basic freedoms in the university" and that "competition among ideas is essential to the vitality of free enterprise," over half had some doubt about their willingness to provide support without interfering in academic policies and practices. Over three-fourths complained of a liberal bias and lack of support for market-based systems among university faculty and students. About one-third said that the economic or political views of faculty are an important factor in corporate decisions to support a university (Magarrell, 1979). Ambivalence of this kind permeates these interinstitutional relationships and creates a strong case for building careful balances into new relationships.

The core of the problem, and the critical element differentiating business–higher education relations eighty years ago from those of today, is that business and education were less equal institutions then, with few goods on either side worth exchanging. They spoke entirely different languages and envisioned for themselves entirely different purposes. Higher education could confer some legitimacy and prestige on those it touched but had few direct benefits of real scale to offer industrialists and politicians. Similarly, business and industry had little to offer higher education other than financial support of a worthy social institution.

During the past thirty years, however, a complex network of relationships has developed, and is still developing, between business and higher education. The interconnections are interpersonal, interinstitutional, and intellectual in nature. The prestige universities are as affected as the community colleges and technical schools. Key factors in the creation of this network are:

• Corporate presence on the boards of trustees of colleges and universities, private and public, and domination of corporate board rooms and planning staff since World War II by college and graduate school trained managers and technocrats

• Expanded corporate educational philanthropy, stimulated in part by the formulation in 1952 of the Council for Financial Aid to Education

• Consultantships and community service projects of faculty members and extensive use of real-world sites and learning experiences for students

• Availability of corporate and union tuition assistance

• Growth of professional associations and their publications as forums for "cultural exchanges" between members of the two sectors

• Ability of community colleges to penetrate the market for all types of occupational training, in part creating that market while transferring costs from employers to individuals and taxpayers

• Improved career guidance, student placement, and employee recruitment processes that attempt to make postsecondary education more of an integrated function for the career advancement of individuals.

Without this intertwining of ideas and people, institutional collaboration would be impossible to achieve. Taken together with common interests in solving economic, political, and technological problems, these relationships form the basis for coalition building (Stauffer, 1980).

Yet all available evidence still reveals the modest influence of these relationships on the present activities of colleges, universities, and corporations. Corporations account for only about 3 percent of campus-based basic research. With a few notable exceptions, few higher education institutions have made off-campus internships, cooperative education, and other experiential learning programs central methods within their curriculum. Career planning and placement information systems are only beginning to have effects. While corporations may stand ready to be used more often as learning sites, their potential is relatively untapped (Lusterman and Gorlin, 1980). Use of tuition-assistance programs by nonmanagement employees rarely exceeds 3 percent of the eligible work force. The corporation that actively encourages management and other employees to pursue continuing education beyond immediate work-related training is exceedingly rare (Charner, 1980; Knox, 1979). The great bulk of corporate human resource education and training thus far is performed in-house or through consultants and very little through campus-corporate programs.

A theme emerges from these observations: Although the relationships between the higher education and business sectors may be complex, they do not yet engage the vested interests of the two sides. We have not yet reached a point where the enrollments of higher education or the profits of corporations have been tied to direct collaborative planning and action. Nor have we reached a point where the benefits and costs of collaborative planning and action have been clearly stated, placed in proportion to the overall missions of the two sectors, and used to develop a comprehensive consensus on the future distribution of education, training, and research in the United States. This is not to say that such linkages are not feasible or not already being tested. Whether they are inevitable or desirable must be left to discussion, which this sourcebook hopes to stimulate.

Current Higher Education–Business Relationships

The changing nature of higher education–business relationships will become more clear through examples of collaboration in each of four functional areas:

1. The production and distribution of *teaching/learning experiences and services*. Which institutions have been and will be responsible for adding economic and other values to human resources?

2. The production and distribution of *new ideas and products*. Who is and will be responsible for basic and applied research?

3. The *flow of human resources* between education and employment. Who will design, finance, and manage (in sum, who will control) information and opportunities for directing individuals into education and work?

4. The process of *strategy development*. Who has been and will be responsible for deliberate planning and communication among policy makers influencing the structure of education and business relationships for the three previous functions?

These four categories are derived from considering the exchanges of resources that higher education and business can offer to each other: people, money, ideas, power, time, places. Can collaborative activities in these four areas produce mutual respect, trust, reliability, and demonstrated results that will benefit individual businesses, higher education institutions, and adult learners?

Teaching and Learning. By shattering the administrative lockstep of the standard degree program, the more innovative community colleges and universities of the past twenty years created within themselves the attitudinal flexibility and administrative agility essential to dealings with other sectors, including employment institutions. Though traditional colleges and universities severely criticized community colleges and nontraditional institutions for adopting such innovations as open enrollment, field experience and cooperative education, assessment of prior learning from life and work experience, and other individualized programs for adult learners, many of those traditional universities today have implemented similar programs and policies.

One might now find on college campuses numerous programs involving the corporate sector (many of the following examples are taken from Bulpitt and Lohff, 1980):

- *Cooperative education programs.* In places like La Guardia Community College in New York City, these programs are campus-wide.

- *College-coordinated apprenticeship and pre-apprenticeship programs.* For example, Dallas County Community College District works with local automobile dealers and with Dallas CETA, construction contractors, and area electrical and carpenters apprenticeship programs.

- *Tuition assistance programs.* For example, Kimberly-Clark Corporation instituted programs with the University of Wisconsin/Oshkosh and other higher education agencies.

- *Industry-services programs.* Many state economic development programs provide vocational training through secondary and postsecondary education institutions, frequently using employer-provided instructors, equipment, and classrooms.

- *Joint curriculum improvement efforts.* Examples include occupational advisory committees, corporate-sponsored in-service programs such as General Electric's Educators-in-Industry Program, and Central Piedmont (Charlotte, N.C.) Community College's Project Upgrade.

- *Small business management training.* Brookdale Community College in New Jersey, for example, houses a Small Business Development Center, a Small Business Institute, and a chapter of the Senior Corps of Retired Executives (SCORE), all funded by the federal government's Small Business Administration.

- *Courses for management.* Miami-Dade Community College and a regional banking corporation developed a for-credit, in-house program using materials, instructors, and media equipment from both college and company. Harvard's Advanced Management Program, conducted since 1943, is the oldest in the nation, with 11,000 graduates.

Meanwhile, corporations have taken steps of their own to fill perceived gaps in the nation's educational services. Few educators appreciate that the teaching/learning function has as venerable a history outside educational institutions as inside them. Corporate education initiatives range from remediation, motivation, and pre-employment skill training to postgraduate learning of the highest level (see Chapter Two by Craig and Evers). Among the more familiar examples are the following:

• The Bell System (AT&T) spent $1.7 billion on employee education and training in 1980.

• Arthur D. Little, Inc. and the General Motors Institute are accredited degree-granting institutions.

• Courses designed and conducted entirely in-house may be evaluated by a credit-recommending authority such as the American Council on Education or the New York State Office of Non-Collegiate Sponsored Instruction (see Chapter Six by Reilly and McGarraghy.

• Control Data Corporation, Chrysler Learning Institute, Singer, and RCA, among many others, compete with schools and colleges as providers of basic, advanced, and employability skill training.

• The increasingly active roles of print and electronic publishers in corporate training and the new markets for home computers, video-cassettes, and videodiscs will have a major influence on future formats for teaching and learning.

The point should be obvious: Higher education does not have an exclusive hold over the teaching/learning function. As business expands its training capacity and hires larger numbers of imaginative, ambitious professionals to staff its training programs, encroachments will be made on the formal education system. But a head-on battle need not happen if the two sides can agree on roles appropriate to their community and economic contexts.

New Ideas, New Products. Historians, sociologists, language instructors, anthropologists, and other humanists, as well as engineers, physicists, chemists, biologists, geographers, and economists all produce ideas. Though strengthening the overall economic and enrollment posture of a postsecondary educaton institution, crucial investments in engineering, business, or basic science education will not hide the fact that, in sharp contrast, the social and aesthetic disciplines must struggle to define their relevance to corporate needs and corporate investments in campus programs.

A recent news article, "Campuses Cementing Business Alliances" (Lohr, Nov. 16, 1980), told of a "global race to spawn new technologies" and "a flow of corporate dollars into university laboratories." Among the examples cited were:

• A Massachusetts Institute of Technology-Exxon ten-year, $7-million program for advanced study of more efficient burning processes

• Harvard and Monsanto's long-term, multimillion dollar program on the biology and biochemistry of organ development

• Johns Hopkins and Estee Lauder's establishment of an institute of dermatology

• Cal Tech's cooperative research program with half a dozen companies—IBM, Intel, and Xerox among them—concerned about advance design work for microprocessors.

Current joint research programs recall the initial boom in defense and space R&D in the 1960s. Peripheral industries clustered around universities (such as Boston's Route 128, northern California's Silicon Valley, and North Carolina's Research Triangle) created consultantships, internships, and small business spinoffs into new technologies. Symbiotic R&D relationships justified area economic development strategies that tied business site selection to the research and management training capabilities of area universities and the technician training capabilities of community colleges.

The trend toward more corporate investment in on-campus research would gain substantial momentum if legislation such as the Research Revitalization Act of 1980 were enacted to provide tax credits for corporate-supported campus research. In November 1980, Congress enacted a bill giving businesses and universities more authority to commercially exploit inventions developed by them under government grants and contracts. These examples of avenues for indirect rather than direct federal investment in "hard" science research may provide the policy direction for future corporate-university R&D efforts.

Flow of Human Resources. To survive, colleges and universities must demonstrate their continuing contribution to the core social function of giving people the skills they need to earn a living and provide social institutions with people capable of performing needed social roles. The flow of human resources, from an institutional perspective, is a three-stage process: intake, treatment and productive use, and transfer to the outside world.

Under the intake category can be included:

• Corporate-sponsored scholarship programs and industry-wide recruitment/scholarship programs, such as the chemical industry's minorities in engineering (ChIME) program

• Higher education-sponsored career information and exploration programs, such as M.I.T.'s Work in Technology and Science project

• Joint information and outreach programs, such as Career Guidance Institutes initiated by the National Alliance of Business and cosponsored by colleges and community organizations

• Intermediary information sources, such as educational brokers and federally sponsored Education Information Centers, which work with employers and higher education

• Corporate programs such as Polaroid Corporation's Tuition Assistance Office.

Within the treatment and productive use stage are numerous examples built around teaching/learning activities such as cooperative education, internships, industry-services, and apprenticeship programs cited earlier. Coordinator positions are an important part of this process, including co-op and industry-services coordinators on campuses and liaison positions within corporations and trade associations, such as Chamber of Commerce and National Alliance of Business regional human resource managers.

Flow of human resources is enhanced by the employer's ability to use the teaching/learning activity as a means of advance assessment and screening of prospective employees, by the learner's ability to develop personal contacts and a work experience resume, and by the higher education institution's ability to reduce its isolation and to establish a credible "track record" with corporate personnel and training departments.

In the transfer, or output, stage can be included the career guidance and placement offices found on almost all college campuses, providers of occupational information such as State Occupational Information Coordinating Committees and corporate developers of occupational information materials and systems, and various local collaborative councils whose purpose is to smooth the movement of individuals between education and work.

Strategy Development. Leadership will be required to move beyond individual examples to a broad consensus on how higher education and business, together with government and labor, can meet the nation's manpower, training, and research needs. Far more than new dollars, leadership is what will make the difference. Far more than rhetoric, effective mechanisms for sustaining communications and collaborative programs are essential to effective leadership.

Three examples of problem-solving mechanisms are collaborative councils, credible projects and programs, and conferences. Collaborative councils speak to the problem of how to maintain leadership communication across the sectors on a particular topic or set of topics over an extended period of time. Credible projects and programs address the problem of how to implement agreements made at leadership levels or how to demonstrate the utility of new services on an experimental basis prior to top leadership involvement. Conferences are valuable for their cumulative effects on network building rather than for their one-time contributions. Taken together with more informal contacts, formal "centers," and coordinator positions within corporations and colleges, these mechanisms are the infrastructure upon which coalitions are formed.

Collaborative councils address the common interests of both sectors:

• The Joint Council on Economic Education was formed in 1947 with business, labor, and education support to assist economic literacy programs throughout the nation.

• The Council on Corporate/College Communications, organized in 1976 by the American Association of State Colleges and Universities and eight major corporations, sponsored campus-based programs, including businessperson-in-residence and faculty-management forums.

• Local and state-initiated industry-education or work-education councils bring together multisector leadership in at least 140 communities nationwide. Networks of councils exist in several states, notably California, Connecticut, Michigan, and New York. Councils are represented by two associations: the National Work-Education Consortium and the National Association of Industry-Education Cooperation.

• Approximately 450 local and state Private Industry Councils (PICs) were created in 1978 under the Comprehensive Employment and Training Act (CETA). Mandated membership includes a business majority and representation from other sectors, including local higher education institutions.

• The Business–Higher Education Forum, organized in 1978 by the American Council on Education, consists of chief executive officers of major corporations and college and university presidents and chancellors. In 1981 the topics on the forum's agenda are energy research, engineering manpower, capital formation, and cooperative R&D.

• The University Advisory Council of the American Council of Life Insurance was established in 1967 as a forum for discussions among college presidents, leaders of education associations, and top executives of the life insurance industry. The council sponsors meetings, programs such as Business Executive in Residence, and conferences on long-term societal issues.

• Secondary and postsecondary education institutions receiving federal Vocational Education Act monies must establish local advisory councils. Local membership is typically weighted heavily toward employers. These councils tend to focus on curriculum issues.

Credible projects and programs are building blocks, the "nuts and bolts," of institutional relationships. Many examples were noted earlier in this article under the teaching/learning, new ideas and products, and human resource flow functions. These are included under strategy development because, when successful, they provide credibility and contacts for subsequent initiatives and are, therefore, integral to long-term planning of intersector strategies. A single example should suffice: In many communities, cooperative education programs are most closely identified with corporate-campus alliances (Wilson, 1980). The responsibilities of employers, students, and faculty are easy to understand, and the rewards are tangible and immediate. A few colleges make the cooperative experience the central point around which curricula, guidance, financial aid, and job placement are provided. Enthusiastic national evaluations resulted in expansion of federal funding for cooperative education and inclusion of co-op students (whether or not economically disadvantaged) among the target groups for whom employers can receive Targeted Jobs Tax Credits (Elsman and Robock, 1979).

Conferences can also be designed as strategy-building mechanisms. For example, the American Association of Community and Junior Colleges, the American Vocational Association, and the American Society for Training and Development jointly sponsored a 1980 conference on "employee training for productivity" with the purpose of opening communications and cooperation among the constituencies of the three groups (Yarrington, 1980). The twelve-year-old League for Innovation in the Community College, a group of seventeen community colleges, provides another example. A June 1980 league conference on cooperative efforts between community colleges and local businesses resulted in a publication describing over 200 linkage projects under way (Bulpitt and Lohff, 1980). In December 1980, the league pursued this theme at an executive retreat for college presidents and top corporate executives.

The point of these examples of mechanisms for strategy development is simple: Recent years have seen increasingly effective talk and action aimed at creating sustained communications between business and higher education. These mechanisms have helped produce ideas, commitments, demonstration projects, and programs with impact locally and/or nationally in each of the four functional areas. What has happened thus far, however, is piecemeal and exploratory.

The Path of Innovation: Toward a System Perspective

Ironically, today's movement toward closer relationships between business and higher education is in many ways a tribute to the success of the reformist ferment within higher education during the past two decades, when innovation had little to do with business. It is interesting that *Change* magazine and The Cornell Center for Improvement in Undergraduate Education's remarkable *The Yellow Pages of Undergraduate Innovations* (1974) did not even use "business cooperation" as an index heading for the 3,000 entries, and "community cooperation" consisted mostly of cooperation among local colleges.

Scattered and sometimes visible higher education projects involving business and other community agencies set valuable precedents; they showed what could be done. But they were incidental to the more pressing issues facing higher education managers, issues that were well documented by the Carnegie Commission (1972), the "Newman" *Report on Higher Education* (Newman and others, 1974), and the Commission on Non-Traditional Study (1973). These studies emphasized the importance of expanded educational opportunities, especially access to higher education for minorities, women, and older adults; diversified instructional techniques and curricular offerings; expanded support services to make full educational opportunity feasible; and administrative restructuring to make educational opportunity possible and meaningful.

The experiential education movement played a leadership role by breaking new ground in identifying new groups of students, new sources of faculty, new learning opportunities in their communities, new formats for interdisciplinary study on campus, new criteria for assessing learner performance, new ways of developing and applying academic standards, and new procedures for working with external organizations and facilitating student and faculty involvement with those organizations (The Cornell Center for Improvement in Undergraduate Education, 1974; Ritterbush, 1972; Carnegie Council on Policy Studies in Higher Education, 1980; and Keeton and Tate, 1978). Questions about who learns, who teaches, and what time, place, money, support services, and administrative procedures are involved—questions thought radical (if thought at all) in 1960—had become commonplace topics by 1980.

What appears to be new about the current decade is that the policy and administrative revolution arising from the reforms of the 1960s and early 1970s in higher education is gaining momentum at the same time as employer and union-based education and training programs are being expanded and reformed.

Employers, too, have experienced a decade or more of expansion and reform of the concepts and practice of corporate education and training. Programs are more numerous and more diverse in scope. Human resource development (HRD) has become a function in its own right, separate from personnel administration. Human resource planning is only now becoming part of overall corporate strategy development. External human resource factors such as the performance of school systems and universities have only recently been widely recognized as direct concerns of corporate leadership rather than as peripheral community relations or philanthropic issues. It is no coincidence, for example, that banking and insurance institutions with community-wide interests have taken special leadership in local and national education and human resource developments.

Cross-cultural mixing and matching of the two sectors is now taking place with some frequency. Assuming these communications result in trust, not suspicion, what do the consequent programmatic relationships imply? How will learners benefit? And who will pay the piper?

From a concept of a "higher education" system, we seem to be headed toward a concept of a lifelong learning system (Fraser, 1980), in which education and training institutions are but one major component. Others are employer institutions; labor unions and professional associations; community services (libraries, educational brokers, and nonprofit special and civic interest groups); and telecommunications (Carpenter, 1980; Charner, 1980; American Council on Life Insurance, 1979; Stack and Hutton, 1980). Though the system is not yet in place, the components are recognizable and the mechanisms, technologies, and concepts are increasingly available. The challenge for innovation in the 1980s will be to put these pieces together in ways that balance creatively the historic tensions created by the enthusiasms and suspicions of leaders and followers in higher education and business.

Business and Higher Education Relationships: Toward Strategy

In education as in politics, the foundation for strategy is demographics (Carnegie Council on Policy Studies in Higher Education, 1980; Crossland, 1980; Frances, 1980). Beyond basic demographics, three factors force realignments in all four functions of corporate–higher education relations. First, the pace of technological innovation has created demands for massive and frequent retraining (perhaps even reeducation) of the nation's labor force. Second, allocations of resources for education are finite and are being redistributed as the average age of the population shifts upward and as alternative claims are made on capital. Third, employers and others perceive failure on the part of education institutions—both secondary and postsecondary—to transmit knowledge, skills, and values needed to survive in a highly competitive world economy. This last argument is especially devastating because almost all education institutions are direct or indirect beneficiaries of tax subsidies. When public confidence decreases, a deadly spiral of declining resources and declining capability sets in. The question is whether higher education will be given enough time and resources to prove that it has the leadership capacity to help employers, unions, and individuals meet the nation's skill requirements during the next decade.

These demographic, technology, resource, and public confidence factors impinge on the relationships between higher education leaders and their corporate counterparts. Both sectors, together with other institutions, will need to come to terms with such issues as:

• *Career mobility.* Will increasing economic constraints limit the financial capability of individuals to change careers and seek retraining? Will opportunities for career mobility exist within corporations as they have in the past decade and will corporations encourage upward career mobility as a motivating factor for formal learning?

• *Investments.* Where will national, corporate, and union policies place investments in human capital as a priority? Will investment decisions assume that human skill development is a necessary precondition of economic and political health? If so, will this assumption be pursued through public and private investments in higher education institutions, through corporate training, through communications media, or through other means?

• *Work patterns.* Will work patterns be made more flexible to accommodate adults? As more adults work, can balance be achieved between the workplace's need for job performance and the individual's need for personal learning and leisure?

• *Consensus.* To what extent will consensus be feasible—whether at community, state, or national levels—on the importance of education and training in the life of the nation? What kinds of agreements will be reached about functional responsibilities appropriate to each sector and the sharing of responsibilities for defining institutional and political policies? What leverage will individual learners have over the formulation of institutional consensus?

• *Tuition costs.* Will increasing costs reduce the numbers of middle-class youths who for a hundred years have been and still are the core of higher education enrollments? Will state and federal tuition subsidies for the "general welfare" be transferred back to individuals as direct costs or to corporations through training budgets? Could costs become so excessive that post–high school job entry might become a prerequisite for higher education studies financed selectively by employers?

This chapter is concerned with how leaders in higher education and business, both at local and national levels, can develop appropriate strategies for collaboration. The major liberal arts and research universities differ in purposes and problems from smaller colleges and community colleges just as major international corporations differ from their suppliers and from local small businesses. Given this diversity in both sectors, are there common needs and resources that form the basis for relationships built on exchanges of substantial benefits to each sector and at acceptable costs?

What higher education today has the ability to deliver and what employers desperately require is skilled labor. A crisis in skilled manpower extends from the highly technical computer, engineering, and basic research occupations to entry-level jobs of almost all kinds in the service as well as manufacturing sectors. Concurrently, the pace of technological change and opportunities for career changes have created a critical need for cyclical "retooling" of working adults in addition to the more traditional preparation of new entrants into the professions.

American managers have historically assumed that "experience is the best teacher" and relied on on-the-job training and experience to correct the inadequacies of the education system. It was expected that new lawyers and engineers as well as clerks and carpenters would have to be brought "up to speed." But more than ever, modern work requires sophisticated preparation. For higher as well as secondary education, therefore, the first challenge is to help learners meet the basic entry requirements of the modern workplace at technician or professional levels. The second challenge is to compete with corporations and many diverse providers in delivering advanced skills to technicians and managers alike. The third challenge, much more difficult still, is to compete with media and a broad mix of other providers in delivering cultural and social education to individual learners.

At the first level, business is likely to rely on support from the formal education sector. At the second level, the two sides will have to cooperate to develop arrangements keyed to local circumstances. At the third level, higher education institutions will have to rely on support from other institutions, notably business and organized labor. For just as corporations and unions receive most of their new workers through the institutional funnel of secondary and higher education, so higher education must look to employers and unions as the institutional connecting points for access to adult learners. Simply put, business leaders and their organizations can offer higher education three strengths: political power, economic resources, and access to adult learners.

In the political arena, business leaders gain their leverage by being net contributors to the wealth of government through direct taxes and, more importantly, through the taxes paid by employees and peripheral enterprises. With organized labor, and to a much greater extent than labor in most states and communities, private employers influence public opinion and public policy on the financing of higher education. Employer and union support for adequate public financing of public higher education, or for appropriate policies regarding private higher education, will be essential in the next decade. But that support will not be forthcoming unless compensating benefits are received.

On the economic side, employers invest substantial resources in employee recruitment and training. What portions of this expense are necessary in-house? What could be spent through higher education organizations? Enrollments and economics have forced college administrators to ask these questions. Responding to every need of the corporation may not be appropriate. But universities, colleges, and technical schools all have some specialties or can develop some that are consistent with their mission and of value to particular employers. The fact that businesses, through their tuition assistance programs for employees, control the nation's largest and least used source of funding for collegiate adult education remains largely unexplored (Charner and others, 1978; Rogers and Shore, 1980). Employers also have research needs. Use of university faculty as consultants and business-funded research are two aspects of this not unusual relationship.

Concerning the access issue, business leaders control (to a degree rarely appreciated by educators) the very structure and content of higher education communications with the vast majority of adult learners. Just as high schools are a funnel point for college access to younger learners, so are employers and unions the natural institutional connecting points to adults. Control over schedules, facilities, location, wages, benefits, career development, and technology already makes employers a major determining factor in the scale of adult enrollments and the breadth of subjects covered. That individuals pursue formal learning despite the rigidity of modern employment patterns only makes one wonder what more flexible and supportive work patterns would bring (Charner, 1980; Shore, 1980). Finally, just as colleges control access to certain kinds of learning, so employers control the number, types, and financial rewards of the jobs whose availability so often motivates learners to defer present income and leisure in preference for academic studies.

Conclusion

One large and generous corporation articulates its criteria for philanthropy and other involvements with higher education: assure a flow of new employees, support basic research in areas related to corporate interests, preserve the quality of the institution, prefer privately controlled colleges and universities as sources of educational diversity, and prefer proximity to company locations (O'Connor, 1980).

The search for business–higher education relationships must start from what the two institutions want now from those relationships. The criteria just listed surely constitute as succinct and typical a list as might be found on the corporate side. On the campus side, the answer may be even more succinct: enrollments and tuition. Concern for consistency with the subject areas and levels of instruction presently offered, for the scheduling of offerings, and for the prerogatives of faculty surely are present, but whether these concerns are seen as obstacles or standards will vary with the beholder.

The bigger problem for the two sectors and for others is to work within the "now" concerns and needs while moving the discussion to anticipation of future concerns and needs. Each sector, each institution, each person will have an independent sense of what these may be. Only through dialogue, research, and actual practice will understandings emerge about the capabilities of the sectors to articulate their needs and assist each other toward solutions.

As business executives and union officials are responsible for the survival of their organizations, so higher education administrators are responsible for theirs. Ultimately, the point of seeking interrelationships is to share that responsibility and, in so doing, ensure the legitimacy and acceptance of each sector's contributions to society. Still at question is whether sufficient numbers of business, higher education, and other institutional leaders perceive these larger needs and the issues around which those needs will be articulated.

Also at issue is whether the interests of individual adult learners will be met through the deliberations and actions of institutions. The interests of learners as consumers of formal educational opportunities rest at present on a combination of their own resources and subsidies of educational institutions derived largely from public tax policies and direct financial aid to institutions and individuals.

The preservation of a consumer perspective in the formulation of public policy may very well depend on political collaboration among the major institutions of business, labor, and education. From this counterbalancing may come more abundant learning opportunities as well as increased understanding of how interinstitutional collaborations may be implemented with due regard for the integrity of diverse institutional missions and structures and for the learning needs and independence of individuals. Without balance and diversity, the outlook would be far bleaker.

Justice Frankfurter once described the "four essential freedoms" of a university as the freedoms: "to determine for itself on academic grounds who may teach, what may be taught, how it should be taught, and who may be admitted to study" (Moynihan, 1980, p. 32). These essential freedoms have indeed been at the core of higher education's integrity as a distinct institution. Yet today they may also describe corporate education and training.

A skeptical view would admit to the risk that the end result of all the efforts described in this volume, if they are carelessly pursued, could be the demise of higher education as an independent and critical enterprise, replaced by an intermeshed human resource subsystem directed by an oligarchical economy and polity. A more positive view of the future of higher education–business collaboration would anticipate enormous opportunities for creative thinking and program development within a vital mix of democratic institutions.

References

American Council on Life Insurance. *Power and Decisions: Institutions in an Information Era.* Washington, D.C.: American Council on Life Insurance, Summer 1979.

Bulpitt, M., and Lohff, J. K. *It's Your Business: Cooperative Efforts Between Community Colleges and Business/Industry.* Phoenix, Ariz.: Maricopa Community Colleges and the League for Innovation in the Community College, June 1980.

Carnegie Commission on Higher Education. *New Students and New Places: Policies for the Future Growth and Development of American Higher Education.* New York: McGraw-Hill, 1972.

Carnegie Council on Policy Studies in Higher Education. *Three Thousand*

Futures: The Next Twenty Years for Higher Education. San Francisco: Jossey-Bass, 1980.

Carpenter, T. *Calling the Tune: Communication Technology for Working, Learning, and Living.* Washington, D.C.: National Institute for Work and Learning, 1980.

Charner, I. *Patterns of Adult Participation in Learning Activities.* Washington, D.C.: National Institute for Work and Learning, 1980.

Charner, I., Knox, K., LeBel, A., Levine, H. A., Russell, L. J., and Shore, J. E. *An Untapped Resource: Negotiated Tuition Aid in the Private Sector.* Washington, D.C.: National Manpower Institute, 1978.

Commission on Non-Traditional Study. *Diversity by Design.* San Francisco: Jossey-Bass, 1973.

The Cornell Center for Improvement in Undergraduate Education and *Change* magazine. *The Yellow Pages of Undergraduate Innovations.* New Rochelle, N.Y.: *Change,* 1974.

Council for Financial Aid to Education. *Corporate Support of Higher Education, 1979.* New York: Council for Financial Aid to Education, n.d.

Crossland, F. "Learning to Cope with a Downward Slope" *Change,* 1980, *12* (5), 18, 20–25.

Elsman, M., and Robock, S. *Federal Hiring Incentives: New Ways to Hold Down Taxes and Training Costs.* Washington, D.C.: National Institute for Work and Learning, 1979.

Feinberg, W., and others. *Revisionists Respond to Ravitch.* Washington, D.C.: National Academy of Education, 1980.

Frances, C. "Apocalyptic versus Strategic Planning." *Change,* 1980, *12* (5), 19, 39–44.

Fraser, B. S. *The Structure of Adult Learning, Education, and Training Opportunity in the United States.* Washington D.C.: National Institute for Work and Learning, 1980

Giamatti, A. B. "Private Character, Public Responsibility." *Yale Alumni Magazine,* 1980, *43* (8), 10–13.

Keeton, M., and Tate, P. J. (Eds.). *New Directions for Experiential Learning: Learning by Experience—What, Why, How,* no. 1. San Francisco: Jossey-Bass, 1978.

Knox, K. *Polaroid Corporation's Tuition Assistance Plan: A Case Study.* Washington, D.C.: National Manpower Institute, 1979.

Lohr, S. "Campuses Cementing Business Alliances." *New York Times,* Nov. 16, 1980, section 12, p. 1.

Lusterman, S., and Gorlin, H. *Educating Students for Work: Some Business Roles.* New York: The Conference Board, 1980.

Magarrell, J. "Corporate Leaders Wary of Federal Aid to Private Universities." *Chronicle of Higher Education,* July 2, 1979, p. 11.

Moynihan, D. "State versus Academe." *Harpers,* 1980, *261* (1567), 31–36, 38–40.

Newman, F., and others. *Report on Higher Education.* Washington, D.C.: U.S. Department of Health, Education, and Welfare, 1974.

O'Connor, D. "What Colleges and Universities Can Expect from Corporations." In Council for Financial Aid to Education, *Corporate Support of Higher Education.* New York: Council for Financial Aid to Education, 1980.

Ravitch, D. *The Revisionists Revised: A Critique of the Radical Attack on the Schools.* New York: Basic Books, 1978.

Ritterbush, P. (Ed.). *Let the Entire Community Become Our University.* Washington, D.C.: Acropolis Books, 1972.

Rogers, A., and Shore, J. *Making Tuition Aid Work for You: An Action Guide for*

Managers, Labor Officials, Workers, and Educators. Washington, D.C.: National Institute for Work and Learning, 1980.

Shore, J. E. *Alternative Work Patterns: Implications for Worklife Education and Training.* Washington, D.C.: National Institute for Work and Learning, 1980.

Stack, H., and Hutton, C. M. (Eds.). *New Directions for Experiential Learning: Building New Alliances: Labor Unions and Higher Education,* no. 10. San Francisco: Jossey-Bass, 1980.

Stauffer, T. M. (Ed.). *Agenda for Business and Higher Education.* Washington, D.C.: American Council on Education, 1980.

Veblen, T. *The Theory of the Leisure Class.* New York: Mentor, 1953. (Originally published New York: Macmillan, 1899.)

Veysey, L. *The Emergence of the American University.* Chicago: University of Chicago Press, 1965.

Wilson, J. W. *Models for Collaboration: Developing Work-Education Ties.* Boston: Cooperative Education Research Center, Aug. 1980. (Mimeographed)

Yarrington, R. (Ed.). *Employee Training for Productivity.* Washington, D.C.: American Association of Community and Junior Colleges, 1980.

Gerard G. Gold is a senior program officer at the National Institute for Work and Learning, a private, nonprofit organization concerned with the development and implementation of education-work policies and practices. He directs the Institute's Industry-Education-Labor Collaboration Project for the U.S. Department of Education.

U.S. employers spend billions of dollars annually on employee training and education. Future directions for this "shadow education system" will depend, in part, on the responsiveness of the traditional education system to employer needs.

Employers as Educators: The "Shadow Education System"

Robert L. Craig
Christine J. Evers

Private and public employers in the United States are making a massive investment in the education and training of their employees—roughly $30 billion annually, according to the American Society for Training and Development (ASTD), whose members develop, conduct, and manage such programs for employers. Employers provide programs of instruction in virtually every job-related knowledge and skill for employees from entry level through management. They employ instructors and other professionals to design, select, deliver, and administer the programs, which often are presented in employer facilities devoted solely to learning activities. Employers evaluate their programs and methods for effectiveness, and a growing number of larger employers' courses are recognized for college credit. Hundreds of tuition assistance programs also are made available by

We wish to thank the following ASTD members for the information they provided through interviews: John S. Jenness, director of human resources planning and development, Consolidated Edison Company, New York; Bart L. Ludeman, former vice-president and human resource development administrator, Lloyds Bank California, Los Angeles, now president of Bart Ludeman and Associates; and Craig D. Musick, training director, Graniteville Company, Graniteville, S.C.

G. Gold (Ed.), *New Directions for Experiential Learning: Business and Higher Education— Towards New Alliances*, no. 13. San Francisco: Jossey-Bass, September 1981.

employers to their employees. In short, employers are the source of what amounts to a growing education system for their employees.

While the major portion of education and training expenditures are made by large corporations, middle-sized and small firms increasingly depend upon both "in-house" education and training and purchased programs or materials to maintain and upgrade the competence of their work forces. It is not unusual for firms with 200 to 300 employees to have their own training program. Public employers—federal, state and local governments—are heavily involved in employee training too. The federal government alone reported 33.3 million hours of training for its over two million civilian employees in fiscal year 1979.

This chapter examines four aspects of the employers' education system: its magnitude and growth; the historical reasons for its development; functions of employee educators and training practices; and potential for business/higher education collaboration based upon employer needs.

Consider some examples of employers' expenditures and efforts:

• The *Bell System* projected a $1.7 billion expenditure on employee education and training for 1980 alone. Some 12,000 courses were being offered in 1,300 locations, with 20,000 to 30,000 of its one million employees involved in training of one-half hour or more on any given day ("Twelve Thousand Courses . . . ," 1980). For 1979, when the Bell System's projected expenditure was $1 billion, costs were allocated as follows: $100 million for developing new training materials or revising old ones; $100 million for "support functions" (research in learning and training; development of cost-effective methods of conducting training; general management/control of the training function); and $800 million for training delivery. The latter included instructor and student salaries, costs of training facilities and other "associated" expenses (Blount, 1980).

• *Consolidated Edison* of New York spent some $5.5 million in 1980 on the formal training and development of its 24,000 employees. That sum did not include at least $672,900 in 1980 tuition assistance expenditures, nor did it include the wages and salaries of trainees. The figure did include salaries for a training staff of over 100. Eighty of these professionals concentrated on technical skills areas such as data processing, power generation operation and mechanics, welding, overhead lines, gas operations, customer services; twenty devoted their time to management development. In 1970 when Con Ed had more employees (26,000), its training budget was far less—roughly $400,000—and most of the employees were trained informally, on the job.

• *Lloyds Bank of California*, with 4,000 employees, had a training/development department budget of about $4 million in 1980. The bank operated four teller schools, ran assessment centers eleven times a year to identify supervisors and managers for promotion and diagnose training needs, and conducted over 180 classes in supervisory training and management development. Only a small portion of the salaries paid to trainees are counted in the $4 million figure, and none of the salaries of most of the instructors—the bank primarily uses its own line people to perform that function. Some $200,000 was expended on internally conducted training-related research. Other large items in the budget were supplies and equipment, consultant fees, and internally produced audiovisuals. Ten years ago, when Lloyd's had 2,500 employees, its budget for training and development activities was between $40,000 and $50,000.

• *Graniteville Company,* a textile manufacturing firm with plants in South Carolina and Georgia, had a one-man "training department" in 1966 to service the training and development needs of 5,700 employees. In 1980 that department had seventy-six training specialists and serviced the needs of 6,800 employees. The director was responsible for the company's operator, vocational-technical, supervisory and management development programs, as well as for its audiovisual production, assessment center, employee orientation, and other support activities, including tuition assistance. The budget was roughly $775,000, including instructors' salaries. The training department operated as a "cost center," recouping certain training costs from operating divisions.

Employer Investment: Magnitude and Motivations

As might be suggested from these examples, a major problem in determining the exact magnitude of employers' growing investment in education and training is lack of uniformity in allocating costs, and in defining the terms used to report them. Willingness to release such information varies as well. These factors reflect the diversity of organizational structures, methods, and policies. Estimates of annual employer expenditures for employee education and training vary widely, ranging from a low of $2 billion (Lusterman, 1977) to a high of $100 billion (Gilbert, 1976). It is no wonder that the term "shadow education system" has been used to describe employer involvement in education and training (Lusterman, 1977).

Our $30 billion estimate, which approximates half of the estimated $65 billion spent in 1980 for traditional higher education, includes expenditures for in-house (employer-provided) education and training—instructors' salaries, hardware and software, training facilities; research, design, planning, administration, and evaluation of the training/development function; tuition assistance for employees; seminars and workshops; consultant services, related travel, and living expenses; correspondence courses and other forms of self-study media; plus indirect cost of overhead allocation. It does not include the costs of wages and salaries to those being trained.

If wage and salary costs for trainees were included, ASTD's estimate of annual employer expenditure would be considerably higher. A soon-to-be published study of employer-sponsored training by Columbia Teachers College Center for Adult Education considered the relationship of wages and salaries to other training costs (Weinstein, 1980). Although reporting much difficulty in obtaining employer costs, and in being able to make meaningful comparison of them, they estimated average training dollar expense to be 37 percent for "classroom costs," 28 percent for "administrative costs," and 35 percent for "participant compensation and organizational facility costs." In the fifteen cases studied, the costs per participant ranged from $146 in one program to more than $15,000 in the most costly program ("New Education-Work Initiatives at Mountain Bell," 1981).

One indication of the growth of the field is that membership in ASTD has doubled in the past decade to over 21,000 national members, with probably another 20,000 holding only local membership in one of ASTD's 127 chapters throughout the United States. The major portion of this growth occurred between 1974 and 1980.

Training has become an industry in itself. Another growth indicator, exhibit space at ASTD's annual conference, has more than doubled to 36,700 square feet in the past five years. A visit to the exposition hall would reveal: companies that make training films as well as those which sell the equipment for employers to make their own films and videotapes; firms that produce audio cassettes, videotapes, projectors, slides, computerized learning systems, and videodiscs; companies that publish technical or business books and packaged learning programs; companies that offer consulting services in virtually every specialty area of employee education and training.

Again, there are no definitive data about the size of the training industry that supplies the vast array of products and services to employer organizations. One believable estimate made recently was that 35 percent to 40 percent of employers' training expenditures were spent externally with the rapidly growing training industry.

Colleges and universities, of course, provide some of these services, but the sparse data now available suggest that the traditional higher education share of this market is small. For example, a 1977 Bureau of National Affairs, Inc. study (Miner, 1977) showed that only 6 percent of the organizations studied used university executive development resources for their supervisory training, whereas 75 percent of them had their own in-house programs. More recent data from The Conference Board ("New Data for Tuition Aid . . . ," 1980) showed company personnel plus vendors and suppliers to the company as major sources of instructors for on-site employee training and education. At least one observer contends that traditional higher education has lost its leadership in continuing education of professionals, citing various statistics to make the point: 3,000 entities offer business and management courses, only 700 of which are colleges and universities; 40,000 business seminars offered to the public annually, excluding college university extension sources and company in-house programs; the American Management Association's 3,200 programs enroll 100,000 annually (Maxwell, 1980).

Employers have assumed a major role as educators for a variety of reasons:

- To compensate for inadequacies of traditional education, not only in basic skills of secondary school graduates, but also to train many college-educated employees who lack abilities in a wide range of generic areas such as communication, decision making, and interpersonal relations
- To cope with economic and social changes that affect the workplace
- To provide upward mobility for employees through training for more technical or managerial responsibility
- To cope with the changes in technology that make job skills and knowledge obsolete
- For proprietary reasons (this is how we want you to do it here) or for competitive reasons (sales training for company-specific product knowledge)
- Because of inconvenience (scheduling, administration, distance) or unavailability of suitable traditional education services.

Not all of these reasons operate simultaneously in affecting employer decisions on education and training. These are simply the most obvious factors. Industries and employers have different characteristics and different needs. Traditional educators should assess employer needs and interests if they want to serve the nontraditional employee education market.

The following brief review of the history of employer involvement in education and training should illustrate two main points. First, need is the basic motivation for employers to assume education and training roles, whether that need is to cope with technological, social, or economic change, to maintain a competitive edge, or to compensate for the inadequacies of traditional education.

Second, employer roles have expanded over a long period from transmittal of basic technical skills to a broad concern for human resource development (HRD), a term that reflects concern for individual as well as organizational performance. Corporations look to the development of their human resources (employees) as an investment necessary to ensure economic success.

Employer History of Meeting Work Training Needs

Employer-provided education and training is nothing new (Steinmetz, 1976). Rules to govern apprenticeship were included in the Code of

Hammurabi some 4,000 years ago. The medieval craft guilds refined this form of training, and of course apprenticeship continues today within the craft-trade union structure and elsewhere. The basic method of apprenticeship training—in which a skilled worker transmits knowledge to a learner by coaching, learner observation, and supervised practice—undergirds much of industrial skills training.

By the 1800s, apprenticeship alone was inadequate to meet America's burgeoning needs for skilled workers. Some vocational/technical schools began to emerge and by 1862 Congress recognized a greater need for training in agricultural and mechanical arts with passage of the Morrill Act establishing land grant universities.

But these efforts were not sufficient, and employers began to establish factory schools. One of the first factory schools was begun in 1872 by Hoe and Company, when that New York City printing press manufacturer established a school to train machinists so the firm could keep up with its expanding volume of business (Steinmetz, 1976). Similar schools were begun by Westinghouse (1888), General Electric (1901), Baldwin Locomotive Works (1901), and International Harvester (1907). Steinmetz (1976) says this became "common practice," with "companies such as Western Electric, Goodyear, Ford, and National Cash Register in the forefront of this educational activity"(p. 6). This development is not surprising when one considers that these firms were developing the technologies that were fueling U.S. industrial growth. The initial goal was to provide entry-level skills. By 1913 there was sufficient activity directed toward this goal that sixty representatives from thirty-four firms established a National Association of Corporation Schools. (In 1920 the group became the National Association of Corporation Training, and three years later, reflecting broadening interest, it became the American Management Association.)

Major developments occurred in 1917—the Smith-Hughes Act authorized the first federal funds for vocational education, and the entry of the United States into World War I resulted in creation of the Emergency Fleet Corporation of the U.S. Shipping Board. In order to train several hundred thousand workers to build a "bridge of ships" to Europe, the new corporation, staffed by private-sector corporate personnel on loan to the government and led by a former vocational school instructor, developed a four-step method for shipyard supervisors to use in training new workers on-the-job. That method—"show, tell, do, check"—was central to much of industrial skills training until World War II (Steinmetz, 1976; McCord, 1976).

The boom years following the war apparently did little to encourage unusual industry training efforts, although correspondence schools did become widely used. During the Depression, management largely filled its needs for workers from among the ranks of unemployed. But Steinmetz identified two training influences emerging from the Depression experience. First, the population became "training-conscious" as a result of widespread handicrafts training offered with federal funding in those years. Second, business recognized that economic recovery would occur only if people could be encouraged to buy their products. The National Society of Sales Training Executives was founded in 1940 to facilitate professional communications in this area.

World War II, with its enormous demands for personnel and materiel, provided a major impetus to training. Roughly two million plant supervisors and foremen learned methods that enabled them to train an unskilled work force—many of whom were women, elderly, or had physical disabilities. Training became an integral part of the supervisory function, and there was a widespread emergence of training directors to coordinate the effort.

ASTD owes its direct origin to a group of training directors in the petroleum industry, who began meeting in 1939 to exchange ideas and experiences. In 1942 training directors at petroleum companies in seven states invited their counterparts in other major industries to become part of a national organization called the American Society of Training Directors (Steinmetz, 1976). Some 200 signed up, and in 1945 the new society held its first annual conference.

Led by industry executives with World War I Emergency Fleet Corporation experience, the Training Within Industry (TWI) Service (later part of the War Manpower Commission) in 1940 began refining years of know-how into three major training programs to be used by plant operating personnel. These were the "J" programs—job instruction training, job methods training, and job relations training—that helped American industry meet its wartime production needs. Later programs were added in job safety training and program development training.

Responding to workers' needs in college-level subjects, Engineering, Science and Management War Training (ESMWT) launched programs in technology and management, conducted by colleges and universities both on and off campus. Steinmetz (1976, p. 11) says that "in many communities they became the forerunners of junior or community colleges," as well as "the strong roots" for the continuing education centers and management training centers that developed later.

Still another World War II effort influenced management development—the assessment center method used during the war to select intelligence personnel for the Office of Strategic Services (OSS). Early attempts to apply the method in business were not successful until American Telephone and Telegraph (AT&T) began a longitudinal study of young managers (1956–60). AT&T used an assessment center process in that study; its methods were the basis for later applications, which proliferated in the 1960s and continue in use today (Bray, 1976).

Partly because of the wartime emphasis on the supervisor's role, as well as the advancement of management concepts by the behavioral sciences, there was increased interest in management development during the 1950s. Supervisory training, perhaps the most prevalent form of employee training today, experienced strong growth during that period. Also, brainstorming techniques and "creative thinking" were common employee training programs. "Human relations training" gained popularity as a way to get people to work together more effectively. This direction continued into the 1960s, with even more emphasis on management leadership styles and communications skills (how to listen, for example). The organization development movement (building teams as opposed to training individuals) became widespread.

The late 1950s and the 1960s were also marked by a rush to "teaching machines and programmed instruction," which probably received wider attention in employee training than in traditional education. Although the faddism of the teaching machines rapidly disappeared, the movement did leave a strong and useful residue of what came to be called instructional system design (ISD) technology, which provides a systematic approach for determining training needs and designing learning experiences to fill those needs. The ISD approach, probably used more often and more effectively in employee education and training than in any other education sector, is undergoing a rebirth as the potential of microcomputers is explored.

Proprietary interests also emerged in training, especially about management, sales practices, or product information. Partly because of this employer attitude, much training for the ranks of supervisors through middle management was (and is) done internally, or at the direction of the employer by the training industry. Many companies developed their own elaborate management training programs with hierarchies of courses and development experiences, including comprehensive assessment centers to select candidates for promotion and to diagnose management development needs.

Basic job skills training at the entry level generally was of less concern in the immediate post–World War II period, probably because there were sufficient numbers of skilled workers who could pass on their knowledge informally, on the job. The exception, of course, was in the emerging new industries characterized by high technology and specialization, such as computers, communications, commercial aviation. Employees needed to be constantly trained in the state of the art as corporations continuously invented it.

As the manufacturing portion of the U.S. economy lost ground in relation to the service industries in the 1960s and 1970s and as large cohorts of youth with value systems different from those of their elders began entering the work force, training in interpersonal relations played a larger role. Basic job skills training for the youthful entrants received renewed emphasis, and remedial education became a concern as well. Employers began to complain—and still are complaining—that basic academic skills are sadly lacking in employees of all levels, that they must reteach reading, writing, and mathematics, as well as subjects such as accounting for MBAs or generic skills such as communication for managers. With the increased entrance of women and minorities into the work force, affirmative action became still another training concern. And as federal regulations affecting business expanded, so in many cases did trainers' roles in familiarizing employees with new requirements such as Occupational Safety and Health Administration safety procedures.

All of these more recent concerns are included in the broad concept of human resource development (HRD), which is concerned with overall competence of the work force. Not confined to hourly employees or to those who produce goods or provide direct services, the HRD concept extends from entry-level employees through top management. It encompasses generic skills that employees at all levels must bring to their job, specific occupation-related skills, and knowledge acquired through traditional education and work. The essential purpose of HRD is to improve organizational and individual performance in the workplace.

Employers view skill acquisition as a continuous process. This is similar to the lifelong learning theme now common in traditional education. The difference is that the employers' primary goal is improved organizational, not just individual, performance.

For example, the current movement known as quality of work life usually falls under the overall concept of HRD. Quality of work life is a broad-based movement encompassing practices such as participative management within work groups, autonomous work groups, restructuring of jobs to give more sense of ownership by individual workers, and other means of building more job satisfaction. The ASTD Quality of Work Life Task Force has defined the concept as "a process for work organizations which enables (their) members at all levels to actively participate in shaping the organization's environment, methods, and outcomes. This value-based process is aimed toward meeting the twin goals of enhanced effectiveness of the organization and improved quality of life at work for employees" (Skrovan, 1980, p. 29).

Also of importance is the growing trend of top management to see HRD as part of the strategic planning process. A recent study showed that chief executive officers ranked manpower planning and development as the most important personnel information ("InSci Poll Results . . . ," 1979), and more large corporations are moving to predict their needs on a systematic basis. Tenneco, for example, requires its vice-presidents to submit a five-year "executive resources" projection along with their five-year business plan.

On the horizon are far greater technological changes and anticipated shortages of skilled workers as America experiences the effects of the
aging of the baby-boom generation. Dr. Benjamin Tregoe, an authority in
corporate strategic planning, contends that human resource development
should be the key function in organizational strategic planning within the
next twenty years ("Effective HRD . . . ," 1980).

Employee Educators: Sources and Activities

As the historical review indicates, many trainers have come from
line operations in the work organization, often asked as supervisors to
transmit their job knowledge and skills to line workers. High-performance
salespeople or mechanics were chosen to train their colleagues, and they
expanded their own skills and knowledges to meet new occupational
challenges. This in part reflects a common belief of many corporate managers that those who actually have performed the job are those best qualified to teach it. In some cases, at least temporary service in training and
development is part of a corporation's management advancement requi-
sites (Nadler, 1980).

With the growth of the HRD field, there was a growing
understanding of what employee educators need to know and be able to do.
Professional groups such as ASTD became sources for the professional
development of employee educators through annual conferences, institutes, workshops, and publications.

Now many institutions of higher learning are offering courses for
employee educators, as well as formal academic programs with certificates
or degrees at the bachelor's, master's, and even doctoral levels. As recently
as five years ago, it would have been difficult to identify more than ten such
academic offerings. But the first national guide to such programs, *ASTD
Directory of Academic Programs in Training and Development/Human
Resources Development, 1981* (American Society for Training and Development, 1981), lists more than 175 offered by seventy-two U.S. colleges and
universities.

In 1978 as a basis for providing more relevant professional
development training for trainers, ASTD published a report on an extensive study of what several thousand employee training practitioners actually did in their jobs. The society's Professional Development Committee
then developed a series of nine basic activity areas representing the overall
functions of the training and development practitioner.

Those areas, encompassing more than one hundred separate activities, are: analyzing needs and evaluating results; designing and developing
training programs and materials; delivering training and development
programs and services; advising and counseling; managing training activities; maintaining organizational relationships; doing research to affect the

training field; developing professional skills and expertise; and developing basic skills and knowledge.

Obviously, the activities of any given training and development practitioner depend upon the needs, goals, and nature of the organization he or she serves and upon the practitioner's place within the organizational structure. Many organizations use only their own internal personnel as instructors and develop most training materials themselves. Others combine external and internal learning methods and sources. Some use "packaged," learner-directed materials. Some practitioners may be responsible for training only entry-level personnel, others only supervisory/management, and many a combination of both.

A study of management training practices published in 1977 by The Bureau of National Affairs, Inc. (Miner, 1977) shed some light on the way 113 organizations, 65 percent with 1,000 employees or more, 35 percent with 1,000 or fewer, conducted such activities. For first-level supervisors, 75 percent operated in-house training programs; nearly 67 percent had such programs for middle managers. "University development programs" had the lowest usage figures reported: only 6 percent used them for supervisors and 39 percent for middle managers. After in-house training programs, the most commonly reported form of management training was "attendance at job-related outside seminars" (66 percent for supervisors; 89 percent for middle managers.) "Self-training/correspondence courses" were used at about the same level in both cases (50 percent for supervisors; 45 percent for middle managers). "Attendance at professional or trade association meetings" was used for middle managers in 96 percent of the responding organizations and in 54 percent for supervisors.

The Conference Board has developed some new survey data regarding "on-site training or education" practices in the manufacturing, utilities, banking, and insurance industries for nonexempt production/operations and office/clerical employees, as well as lower-level exempt employees. Preliminary figures revealed that the most common training method used was "planned on-the-job training"—at least 73 percent of the companies reported this for the nonexempt categories and 61 percent for the exempt. "Lecture, demonstration and group discussion" was the next most frequently used method overall—45 percent for production/operation, 59 percent for office/clerical, and 76 percent for exempt employees—with the next most frequently reported method, for production operations alone, "apprenticeship" at 52 percent ("New Data for Tuition Aid . . . ," 1980, p. 2).

At least 37 percent of the companies reported using full-time company instructors for training all three employee categories, while at least 50 percent used personnel department employees on a part-time bases. Eighty percent of the companies reported that they used foremen, supervisors, and other company personnel to train production/operations employees; for office/clerical and nonexempt employees, the figures were 60 percent and 54 percent respectively. At least 24 percent of the firms reported they used vendors and suppliers to the company in training all three employee categories. To train exempt employees, 48 percent of the companies reported they used "consultants or other outside private training specialists," while 9 percent reported use of "vocational, technical, or business school teachers" and 27 percent said they used "university or college professors."

A major difference between employee education and traditional education is the employee educator's emphasis on assessing needs. Most employee education and training is directed toward a specific purpose— improving job and other organizational performance. Employee educators devote considerable effort to determining what kinds of program content actually will improve performance. In ASTD's (Pinto and Walker, 1978) study report of professional training activities, those activities which dealt with determining training needs clearly were clustered at the high end of the survey response.

Using the instructional system design approach, training needs are identified through analysis of jobs, tasks, performance deficiencies, quality control data, sales data, and any other relevant indicators of performance. The purpose of the training program becomes providing the knowledge and skills that will produce the desired performance. Results of the program then are evaluated and analyzed to determine if the performance goals have been met. Feedback can be fairly immediate because performance deficiencies in certain jobs tend to be obvious. The employee educator can make any necessary adjustments or develop another approach.

This needs assessment approach probably is a major factor in the relatively low usage of traditional higher education programs and resources in employers' training and development programs. As we pointed out earlier, if higher education wants to increase employer utilization of its programs, educational institutions must make an effort to identify employers' needs and increase their responsiveness to them.

Business–Higher Education Collaboration

There are many compelling reasons for employers and educators to seek a whole new order of collaboration. The nation needs a skilled, competent work force. The investment that employers make in skill development is becoming an increasingly significant factor in the price of goods and services. Schools and colleges are facing drastic change because of falling enrollments and criticism of quality performance. Obvious benefits would accrue to all—schools, employers, individual students and workers, and the nation—if industry and education would turn some considerable attention to collaboration in serving work-force training and education needs.

Despite a great deal of rhetoric and some fine examples of effective collaboration, the need for better relations between traditional and employee educators still must be addressed. The task of meeting the educational needs of today's work-force is larger than either can easily accomplish alone. In fact, the roles of educators and employers actually are very little in conflict. For example, there are substantial needs for continuing education and training for the employees of small businesses, which account for most of the nation's jobs. Yet a small business usually does not have the economy of scale to provide its own employee education and training. This kind of need presents opportunities for local educational institutions to work with local employers and their employees. Community colleges have been foremost in meeting such needs, but the overall demand is large and, to a great degree, still unserved.

It is essential to start from a local perspective with an assessment of local needs, perhaps for a specific industry group. A small community in the Southwest may have vastly different needs from a large Northeastern city. And education-work relationships in health care may be vastly different from those in electrical engineering.

Recently ASTD's National Issues Committee commissioned Dr. James W. Wilson of the Cooperative Education Research Center at Northeastern University to develop some principles of how education-work relations might be improved. Wilson identified five simple interrelated elements necessary for effective relations between business and education: (1) both sides must be convinced that they can solve real problems and fill real needs; (2) specific problems must be addressed (simply having meetings will not work); (3) someone, on either side, must reach out to the other side; (4) there must be a productive working phase in the process; and (5) the effort must be reviewed and evaluated for results (Wilson, 1980).

Some of the specific activities Wilson suggests include: student involvement at the work site; continuing liaison and review of relationships; on-going information exchange and joint planning; exchange of faculty and practitioners between campus and work site; applied research by academicians in work-site environments; joint planning and conduct of continuing education. He stresses that education-work problems are addressed most effectively after the educator and the employer have come to know each other personally through professional contacts.

The following examples of collaboration show that it can be done.

• Fairchild Industries and the University of Maryland have launched a graduate level partnership designed to lead to a master's degree in electrical engineering in two years with an emphasis on systems engineering, communications, and software engineering. This Fairchild Scholars Program enables fourteen participants to take graduate courses at the university two days a week and work three days a week at Fairchild Space Electronics Company or at its partnership subsidiary, American Satellite Company. Participants receive a full scholarship from Fairchild for their graduate education costs and are paid by Fairchild for their work, with all benefits of regular employees. The partnership program was initiated by Fairchild, which views it as a "dramatic step in finding a potential solution to the critical shortage of leaders in science and technology" (University of Maryland/Fairchild Industries, Nov. 3, 1980).

• Mountain Bell Telephone Company in Colorado is working with colleges, universities, and technical schools throughout its eight-state service area to introduce telecommunications-related courses such as pole climbing, cable splicing, computer programming, and service representative training into their curricula. Behind the move is the belief that many students subsequently will apply for positions at Mountain Bell, with their initial training completed. At the same time, current employees are expected to enroll to gain additional skills for future promotion and Mountain Bell has expanded its tuition assistance program ("New Education-Work Initiatives at Mountain Bell," 1981).

• The Technical Education Colleges (TEC) system of South Carolina has embarked upon a Design for the Eighties program to meet changing needs for vocational skills. TEC leaders visited a wide range of companies and universities both in South Carolina and out of state to gather first-hand knowledge about what skills were needed and to develop commitments for collaboration. They found, in many cases, that theirs was the only state that had approached the companies to assess needs ("South Carolina 'TEC' Schools . . . ," 1980).

• The Piedmont Area Evening Degree Association in North Carolina is a new consortium of nine businesses (Fairchild Industries, Gravely, Hanes Corporation, ITT Grinnel, North Carolina National Bank, Piedmont Aviation, Schlitz Container Division, Wachovia Bank and Trust, and Westinghouse) that offer undergraduate evening courses at their plant sites using the faculty and curricula of High Point College ("New Education-Work Consortium . . . ," 1980).

The essential point behind these examples is that the traditional and employee educators involved are addressing needs together. To do that, they have had to communicate those needs to each other. Lack of good communication tends to reinforce a lot of mythology on both sides, such as "educators don't want to cope with change" or "employers only care about training for specific jobs within their own organization." Probably the most frequent criticisms of traditional education heard from employee educators are lack of basic skills, curricula not relevant to current needs, and unrealistic career expectations of entry-level people just out of school. Traditional educators have been heard to express fears about a dilution of academics and a loss of academic freedom. The only way for the concerns of both groups to be dealt with effectively is for them to explore education-work needs jointly to determine their relative roles and areas for collaboration.

One encouraging indicator is the growing collaboration of some of the educational societies, most based in Washington, D.C., with constituencies involved in preparing people for jobs and careers. A good example is the 1980 Assembly on Industry-Education Cooperation, held at the Wingspread Conference Center in Wisconsin and sponsored jointly by the American Association of Community and Junior Colleges, the American Society for Training and Development, and the American Vocational Association. One result of the assembly was a series of recommendations on behalf of the members of all three associations, directed to both the national and local levels. Some of those found in the meeting report, *Employee Training for Productivity* (Yarrington, 1980), were:

- The assembly endorsed the "investment" approach (Striner, 1980), which in essence holds that "continuing education and training of the labor force—or human resource development—is an absolutely necessary investment in the nation's future" (pp. 26–27).
- "There must be a national commitment to continuing education programs for occupational upgrading, retraining, or advancement, with shared financing by government, industry, and individuals" (p. 27).
- "There is a need for a workable national policy that addresses human resource development and increased productivity" (p. 27).

ASTD has also held two invitational conferences for higher education representatives on the "Academic Preparation of Practitioners in Training and Development/Human Resource Development," one in 1979 and another in 1981. The latter dealt extensively with the need for academic programs to prepare training practitioners with the skills, knowledge, and abilities to meet the real work needs of present and future employees.

Still another area of potential collaboration lies in tuition aid programs, perhaps the best-known tie between employee education and higher education. Such programs actually are used very little, despite the fact that most large employers offer some form of assistance to pay for courses taken outside of the organization—80 percent to 90 percent in the many studies we have seen (for example, the 1980 data from The Conference Board ("New Data for Tuition Aid . . . ," 1980).

Often 5 percent or fewer of eligible employees participate in such programs. All the reasons for this lack of participation are not clear, although there are many contentions about the "barriers," depending upon the viewpoint of the group. Employee educators often say that the courses are not appropriate. Pro-labor groups sometimes say that management does not provide enough incentive or support. And employees often cite situational barriers, such as lack of time, child care, or transportation (Cross, 1981).

Still another barrier, an unfavorable tax situation for employees who wanted to participate, was alleviated significantly by passage of the Employer Educational Assistance provisions of the 1978 Revenue Act. ASTD and its members led the effort to secure enactment of these provisions, along with employers, unions, and traditional education groups. The provisions eliminated previous Internal Revenue Service requirements that employer education assistance that did not relate directly to the employee's present job had to be considered taxable income to the employee.

The 1978 law excludes virtually all employer education assistance (tuition aid and employer-provided courses of instruction) from employee income tax if employers' plans qualify as being nondiscriminatory and meet several other requirements. The provisions expire at the end of 1983, and we hope that Congress will extend them. But both employer and employee concerns and needs relative to traditional education's offerings still must be addressed by academic institutions if employees are to increase their voluntary participation in tuition aid programs.

Indications are that employers will assume more and more responsibility for educating and training their employees for job and career-related purposes. Technological advances, concern for productivity, and international and domestic competition demand that employers look more closely at the competence of their work forces.

Higher education should have increasing opportunities to build new markets with the nation's employers through better assessment of employers' needs. While a vast in-house employer education system is already in place and growing, the educational needs of the next decade are enormous, and will demand the best efforts of employers and educators working together.

References

American Society for Training and Development. *Professional Development: A Self-Development Process for Training and Development Professionals.* Madison, Wisc.: American Society for Training and Development, 1979.
American Society for Training and Development. *ASTD Directory of Academic Programs in Training and Development/Human Resources Development, 1981.* Madison, Wisc.: American Society for Training and Development, 1981.
Blount, W. F. Statement, U.S. Senate Committee on Labor and Human Resources hearings on *Workplace and Higher Education: Perspective for the Coming Decade, 1979.* Washington, D.C.: U.S. Government Printing Office, 1980.

Bray, D. W. "The Assessment Center Method." In R. L. Craig (Ed.), *Training and Development Handbook.* New York: McGraw-Hill, 1976.

"Effective HRD Will Be Key to Strategic Planning." *National Report for Training and Development,* June 12, 1980, pp. 2–3.

Gilbert, T. F. "Training: The $100 Billion Opportunity." *Training and Development Journal,* Nov. 1976, pp. 3–8.

"InSci Poll Results: CEOs Indicate Manpower Planning Will Be the Critical Personnel Change of the '80s." *InSide Human Resource Management,* Oct. 1979.

Lusterman, S. *Education in Industry.* New York: The Conference Board, 1977.

McCord, B. "Job Instruction." In R. L. Craig (Ed.), *Training and Development Handbook.* New York: McGraw-Hill, 1976.

Maxwell, J. F. "Who Will Provide Continuing Education for Professionals?" *AAHE Bulletin,* Dec. 1980, pp. 1, 6–8, 16.

Miner, M. G. *Management Training and Development Programs, PPF Survey No. 116.* Washington, D.C.: The Bureau of National Affairs, Inc., 1977.

Nadler, L. *Corporate Human Resources Development.* New York: Van Nostrand Reinhold/American Society for Training and Development, 1980.

"New Data for Tuition Aid and On-Site Training, 1964-1979." *National Report for Training and Development,* Oct. 10, 1980, pp. 1–2.

"New Education-Work Consortium in North Carolina." *National Report for Training and Development,* Sept. 12, 1980, pp. 2–3.

"New Education-Work Initiatives at Mountain Bell." *National Report for Training and Development,* Jan. 23, 1981, pp. 1–2.

Olson, E., and Ellis, J. B. "Academic Preparation of HRD Practitioners." *Training and Development Journal,* May 1980, pp. 76–83.

Pinto, P. R., and Walker, J. W. *A Study of Professional Training and Development Roles and Competencies.* Madison, Wisc.: American Society for Training and Development, 1978.

Skrovan, D. J. "A Brief Report from the ASTD Quality of Work Life Task Force." *Training and Development Journal,* March 1980.

"South Carolina 'TEC' Schools Responding to Changing Needs." *National Report for Training and Development,* Oct. 24, 1980, pp. 1–2.

Steinmetz, C. S. "The History of Training." In R. L. Craig (Ed.), *Training and Development Handbook.* New York: McGraw-Hill, 1976.

Striner, H. E. "The Joint Role of Industry and Education in Human Resource Development." In R. Yarrington (Ed.), *Employee Training for Productivity.* Washington, D.C.: American Association of Community and Junior Colleges, 1980.

"Twelve Thousand Courses in Bell System Training!" *National Report for Training and Development,* June 26, 1980, p. 3.

University of Maryland/Fairchild Industries. "A New Partnership Established Between Business and Education." Press release, University of Maryland/Fairchild Industries, Nov. 3, 1980.

Weinstein, L. "Employers as Sponsor." In R. E. Anderson (Ed.), *The Costs and Finance of Adult Education in the United States.* New York: Teachers College, Columbia University, forthcoming.

Wilson, J. W. *Models for Collaboration: Developing Work-Education Ties.* Washington, D.C.: American Society for Training and Development, 1980.

Yarrington, R. (Ed.). *Employee Training for Productivity.* Washington, D.C.: American Association of Community and Junior Colleges, 1980.

Robert L. Craig is vice president, government and public affairs for the American Society for Training and Development. He is editor of the Training and Development Handbook and of ASTD's National Report for Training and Development *newsletter.*

Christine Evers was formerly associate editor of the National Report for Training and Development. *She was founding editor of the* Manpower and Vocational Education Weekly *and* Health Manpower Report *newsletters for Capitol Publications, Inc.*

Effective linkages between universities and industry
require clear-headed analysis of institutional goals,
carefully designed "boundary-spanning" structures,
and a mix of incentives appropriate to each
organization.

Academia and Industrial Innovation

Elmima C. Johnson
Louis G. Tornatzky

A widely held view is that the U.S. economy is not presently performing as well as in prior decades and, moreover, that "technological backwardness" may be a significant part of the problem. As stated in a National Science Foundation (NSF) report (1978): "In terms of growth in GNP and productivity, the U.S. economy has performed poorly during the last ten years compared to the twenty years after World War II. Insufficient R&D and technological innovation have been cited as possible contributors to unsatisfactory U.S. economic progress" (p. 28). This general decline in productivity growth has been attributed in part to a decline in three innovation-related factors: knowledge resulting from research and development (R&D), informal innovations in plants, and the rate of diffusion of technological advances (Cordes, 1980).

The picture that emerges, while not overwhelming in its pessimism, is sufficiently serious to warrant looking at some institutional problems in domestic innovation. Aside from the more traditional concerns with tax, patent, and regulatory policy, there is increasing interest in the role of

The views expressed in this paper are entirely those of the authors and do not represent official policy of the National Science Foundation.

G. Gold (Ed.), *New Directions for Experiential Learning: Business and Higher Education—Towards New Alliances*, no. 13. San Francisco: Jossey-Bass, September 1981.

universities in the process of industrial innovation. To many, the university is seen as a crucial link in the industrial process of innovation. Given the university's principal activities in research and training, what problems and issues is it contending with to meet the demands for technological change?

The University Role in Innovation: Issues and Problems

The Ideal. A common, perhaps prevailing view of innovation is that activities move rather linearly from basic research, to applied research, to development, to marketing and dissemination. For nearly thirty years, the university's role has been primarily to conduct basic research, and it is widely assumed that this research provides a knowledge base that industry and government utilize. Vannevar Bush (1945) gives a classic statement of this view: "The publicly and privately supported colleges, universities, and research institutes are the centers of basic research. They are the wellsprings of knowledge and understanding. As long as they are vigorous and healthy and their scientists are free to pursue the truth wherever it may lead, there will be a flow of new scientific knowledge to those who can apply it to practical problems in government, in industry, or elsewhere" (p. 12).

However, this ideal model of a linear and unidirectional flow of information between universities and industry has not gone unchallenged. As Mogee (1979), states it: "In real life, the progress of an innovation is never that straightforward. Sometime stages are shortened, skipped, or overlapped. Sometimes a retreat must be made to more fundamental work. The activities may occur in different organizations or different countries, involve different persons, and long periods of time may elapse between activities. There are frequently multiple paths of activity leading to an innovation. All this adds up to a complex and uncertain process" (p. 3).

Even when post hoc analyses have found basic research ultimately leading to industrial innovation, the time lags have been considerable, as illustrated by Project Hindsight (Sherwin and Isenson, 1967); Project Traces (ITT Research Institute, 1968); and some case studies by Battelle Memorial Institute (1973). When the use of basic research findings in industry involves a gap of up to twenty years it is moot whether one can speak of a university-industry interaction in any meaningful sense. One other illustrative finding is worth noting. Allen (1977), in a review of the use of university research literature by engineers, found that textbooks were the most frequently used source. There was very little use of scientific journals or reports per se, suggesting that the state of the art in basic science may have only a limited relationship to normative practice in industry.

Another widely held belief is that the university is the optimum place to perform basic research. The increased funding of university basic research by the government and industry, coupled with a decrease in both government and industry funds for industry basic research, implies that both of these sectors believe universities should be the primary performer. Mogee (1979) questions this assumption, pointing out that often the best basic research is performed in a few top institutions and a small number of outstanding industrial laboratories, such as Bell Labs, General Electric, Dupont, and International Business Machines. Indeed, industry performance of basic research may be more efficient and effective because of their understanding of their needs and the potential commercial value of the research (National Science Foundation, 1978).

University Training Activities. A commonly held assumption is that "a large part of the effect of university activities upon industrial innovation is made through the education of scientists and engineers" (Mogee, 1979, p. 12). Yet a number of questions have recently been raised regarding the effectiveness of universities in carrying out this function.

One is whether universities are training science and engineering personnel in sufficient numbers to meet future demands. There are already shortages of trained personnel in computer science, many engineering fields, and subdisciplines of the physical and biological sciences (National Science Foundation, 1980). The rising costs of higher education may further reduce the numbers of science graduate students. A related question is whether colleges have adequately explored sources of qualified students, given that women, minorities, and the physically handicapped are underrepresented in science and engineering programs (National Science Foundation, 1980, p. 5).

The quality of training received by science and engineering personnel is also being reviewed. There are severe shortages of qualified faculty members in the engineering and computer professions because industry is luring away faculty. This has reduced the training capability of universities, as has a lack of updated laboratory equipment, especially for undergraduate instruction.

Concern has been also expressed about the focus of education. Baer (1980) points out that in spite of the success of the Innovation Centers sponsored by NSF, some studies have questioned the ability or interest of universities in fostering entrepreneurial traits in their students. Also of concern is the university's role in continuing education of science and engineering personnel. Current efforts are scattered among colleges, industry, and professional societies with little coordination (National Science Foundation, 1980).

The foregoing discussion was not designed to discourage university-industry transactions but to illustrate that university-industry relationships may be more complex and less predictable in their ostensible benefits than is generally assumed. A much more disaggregated look at specific transaction procedures and programs is needed.

There is a long history of university-industry interactions, much of it mediated by the federal government. As early as 1862, the Morrill Act established land grant colleges, marking the birth of the agricultural extension system, with its well-articulated technology transfer aspects.

World War II brought an unprecedented coupling of business and academic talents in support of national defense, with the most obvious example of this collaboration being the Manhattan project. Some have argued that this period marks the watershed of university-industry relations, and Shapero (1979), for one, believes that the only convincing evidence that university research can stimulate industrial economic activity comes from university-industry cooperation on national defense projects during the two world wars.

The post–World War II era marked the beginning of large-scale federal funding to universities for basic research. In turn, industry efforts moved from basic to applied research and development activities (Brown, 1980). Drucker (1979) has argued that the increase in federal funding for university research following World War II changed the direction of university training and employment as well as its research priorities. As he puts it: "grantsmanship rapidly became the most prized and the most accomplished of the liberal arts. And where industry, whenever it offered support, had the insulting habit of expecting results, government, or so it seemed, was willing to support the scientist for science's sake" (p. 808).

Interaction between universities and industry continued through the 1960s, although on a reduced level. Traditional mechanisms included consultancies, unrestricted research funding by industry for universities, employment of graduates by industry, and interaction via technical meetings, visiting professorships, and advisory committee memberships (Brown, 1980).

University-Industry Relations: Integrating Concepts

Given the history of university-industry interactions, the problems and issues pertaining to, and the general concern with, technological change and productivity, what might be the basis for more stable and productive university-industry exchanges? We hope to answer this question on two levels: by providing a (1) conceptual overview of university-industry interaction as an "exchange" system and (2) some current illustrative examples of linkage systems.

To talk meaningfully about university-industry interactions one needs to talk about the exchanges that take place and about the relative benefits that accrue to each party (Levine and White, 1961). Organizations receive input from their environments, do things with or to it, and transmit the results to other organizations. For example, university inputs include money, buildings, students, laboratory facilities, and trained faculty. Products include basic and applied knowledge, trained students, and cultural uplift. Industries, in turn, need inputs of capital, raw materials, trained personnel, and particularly important for this discussion, knowledge. Outputs are commercial products and processes, some of which represent new technologies and innovations.

Within this framework of exchange, much of the interorganizational literature has tried to identify various factors that are related to greater or lesser interaction. In the remainder of this section, we will focus on three types of such factors: (1) goal congruity and compatability, (2) boundary-spanning structures, and (3) organizational incentives and rewards.

Goal Congruity and Compatibility. Organizations exist to accomplish certain ends or goals. When one organization interacts with another organization, there are varying degrees of goal similarity and goal compatibility. There is evidence in the literature to suggest that the degree of match or mismatch is related to the amount and success of interaction (Reid, 1969; Levine and White, 1961; Tornatzky and Lounsbury, 1979).

For example, universities and industries may share the goal of increasing the knowledge base in a scientific field (albeit for different reasons). They may, in turn, have compatible goals, such as producing trained scientists (the university) and hiring trained scientists and engineers (industry).

Other goals and objectives may be less similar or compatible. For example, industry is primarily interested in commercializing products and processes for profit and is thus by definition more interested in relatively short-run applications; universities (at least in recent decades) have emphasized basic research, discipline-bound science, and the norms of academic inquiry.

Boundary-Spanning Structures. "Interactions" between university and industry are not an abstraction. They typically involve real people, things, and ideas. As such, they must occur in a defined space, time, and setting. Operationally speaking, university administrators and industry executives should probably devote as much time to the organizational design of the units involved in transactions as they do to the scientific and technological content of what is being exchanged.

In the parlance of organization theory, we are talking about "boundary-spanning" units. Depending upon what is being exchanged, these structures could be part of the university or part of the industry firm, or they could occupy some "organizational space" in between. For example, one transaction typically involves the movement of trained students to industrial employers. The boundary-spanning units involved are typically a placement service situated in the university and the personnel units of industry. The organizational design problem becomes the extent to which these units are sufficiently articulated and extended into one another's milieu, such that they really do interact.

Another type of boundary-spanning unit would be involved in an interaction such as a joint research project. Here the organizational home might be a university-based research institute, an industrial lab, or some jointly administered and geographically neutral setting. In contrast to the previous example, the logistical-operational issues here are typically much more involved concerning issues such as intellectual property rights, funding arrangements, selection of research topics, and the like.

One often neglected organizational design issue is the necessity to legitimate and structure the sub-rosa university-industry interaction that is already going on. In most universities, a great deal of informal interaction, often in the form of consulting, is transacted. If universities are interested in promoting and managing university-industry interaction, they would be well advised to provide structures for such activity to occur.

Firm size is also an important consideration in the design of university-industry boundary-spanning units. There is a considerable literature—some anecdotal and some empirical—suggesting that the small firm is heavily involved in innovation, productivity, technological change, and employment creation (Gellman, 1977; Birch, 1979; Abernathy and Utterback, 1978). Planning university-industry linkages that do not take into account the special role of the small firms is ill informed. Unfortunately this introduces logistical difficulties. It is much easier to structure interactions with a few large firms and ignore the numerous, often informal, relations with small firms.

This section has been written using the language of organizational "structure." Equally important are the processess that nest within those structures. For example, there are empirical data (Tornatzky and others, 1980) and practical experience to suggest that information exchanged via person-to-person interaction is more readily assimilated. There are also data to suggest (Allen, 1977; Souder, 1978) that research activity is more productive amidst certain organizational processes than others.

Finally, some minimal degree of geographic propinquity is important to effective exchanges. Universities that are rural and isolated are not likely to develop viable boundary-spanning units, since the span is too wide in a practical sense. Similarly, industrial firms (particularly small companies) that are not adjacent to universities or do not have resources to support travel are not likely to be picked up in innovation networks.

Organizational Incentives and Rewards. Organizational goals and objectives operate at the macro level, as already discussed. Yet these and other goals also operate at a micro level through incentives and rewards (and disincentives and punishments) for individuals involved in university-industry interactions. In designing and implementing collaborative efforts, university administrators and industry executives need to ensure that individual rewards are built into participation.

To illustrate, the reward system in academia is typically centered around promotion and tenure decisions, and to a lesser extent salary. The performance criteria for bestowing these rewards concern scholarly publication, teaching, research, and so forth. Opportunities for accomplishing these objectives need to be obtainable for faculty, via participation in university-industry interactions. Similarly, participation by industry personnel should be a high-status activity and a legitimate route for corporate upward mobility.

These issues bring to focus an irreconcilable problem. Although personnel involved in boundary-spanning activities are different in the sense that the tasks that they perform are at variance with other organization members, they are still part of, and drawn from, the larger organization. They are thus subject to the norms and reward systems of two, perhaps incompatible, subgroups of the parent organization. The individual in this situation can get caught by conflicting role demands and reward systems. In effect, intra-organizational boundary spanning needs to be implemented in the parent university and industry organizations.

Seen in terms of this analysis, a typology of the various university-industry transaction mechanisms could be constructed, including the following factors: What is being exchanged? What organizational goals and objectives are being served, or not served, and what is the similarity and compatibility? What explicit or implicit structures are the setting for the exchanges? and What incentives "motivate" individual actors? These factors could be of some assistance in considering the next section.

Examples of University-Industry Linkage Systems

A variety of university-industry linkage mechanisms have been initiated over the years. They have involved public and private institutions, different types of industries, and several individual or combined sources of funds (industry, federal, state, and local levels of government, trade associations, private foundations). Brodsky, Kaufman, and Tooker (1979) have attempted to categorize these mechanisms, and the result is a list of sixteen types of activity, ranging from corporate-funded university research to consultancies and continuing education programs. It is beyond the scope of this chapter to detail all examples of interactions within each subcategory. However, a few of the most successful programs, as well as several innovative projects, have been selected for discussion. Our discussion will attempt to continue the framework developed at the close of the previous section.

The M.I.T. Polymer Processing Program. The M.I.T. Polymer Processing Program was one of three centers established under the

National Science Foundation (NSF) University Industry Cooperative Research Centers Experiment in 1973. Two other centers were established, at North Carolina State University (furniture industry) and the Mitre Corporation (utility companies) respectively. The M.I.T. program has been the most successful in terms of eliciting industry support, gaining acceptance by the university, and producing tangible results.

The program, which began with $500,000 in seed money from NSF, currently involves twelve firms that pay "membership" fees ranging from $29,000 to $100,000 per year, depending on their size and involvement. Over $500,000 is contributed to support approximately twenty-five primarily applied research projects (Prager and Omenn, 1980). Industrial participants include Eastman Kodak, General Motors, Goodyear, ITT Corporation, and Xerox (Baer, 1980). M.I.T. staff, faculty, and students meet quarterly with member firms to discuss problems, strategies, potential research projects, and results. There are also many informal and ad hoc meetings.

Although the firms suggest research projects, M.I.T. makes the final decision on projects to be initiated. Some appeal to the academic norm of unbridled inquiry is probably operating here. Research results are first shared with the firms to give them an opportunity to develop the ideas. Publications are encouraged (although they may be delayed) as rewards for faculty. A committee of member firms and M.I.T. staff advises on policy matters including fees and patent policies (Goldblith, 1979). All patents are owned by M.I.T., which can license member and nonparticipating firms. Two patents have been issued; eight are pending (Brodsky, Kaufman, and Tooker, 1979). Royalties are shared based on annual firm contributions (Prager and Omenn, 1980).

The university and the member firms profit from this program in a number of ways. "MIT views this program as an excellent learning experience for students; a stimulus for faculty and students to innovate, a means of rapid technology transfer from research to application, a stimulus for broader university-industry interaction, and a means of opening up new disciplines. Industry benefits from new ideas and processes, a source of competent manpower at relatively low cost, timely assessment of current industrial practices, and having a bases for comparative evaluations of internal R&D" (Prager and Omenn, 1980, p. 382). The program's success is attributed in part to the director's excellent academic credentials and strong ties with industry. His leadership is seen as having helped to dispel the university's initial doubts about the program's academic quality (Baer, 1980). The program is currently supported solely by industry and its future success seems likely.

Harvard-Monsanto Research Project. An example of corporate funding of university basic research by a single firm is the Harvard University-Monsanto Corporation program begun in 1975. Monsanto has agreed to provide $20 million over a twelve-year period for basic cell research on the biochemistry and biology of organogenesis. Monsanto initated this project for a simple reason. Although it has a highly developed chemistry research program, the firm does not have expertise in biology research. As a result of its long-range planning, Monsanto decided to commit resources to Harvard to explore this field while developing its own expertise in this area.

A charter agreement allows Harvard to use the funds for any project that fits under the general goals of the program. Currently the money supports the work of personnel from several disciplines and departments. Each partner contributes specific resources to the relationship. Harvard provides a knowledge base in this field, personnel, and training. Monsanto suggests research directions and provides laboratory facilities and equipment. In effect, Harvard controls the research phase, while Monsanto controls the development and marketing phases (Prager and Omenn, 1980).

Patent and publication rights were spelled out in detail in the charter agreement. Specifically Monsanto controls its own results and has exclusive license to all Harvard inventions developed under this agreement for a specified time. There are two restrictions on the disclosure of activities: Each partner can publish its own results only after first informing the other, and neither can disclose information gained from the other. Harvard receives royalties from all patents but has waived royalties from initial sales. An established advisory board reviews these and other policy issues (Prager and Omenn, 1980). Although no specific products have been marketed to date, the research looks promising.

Consulting Relationships: General Issues. One of the oldest and most widely practiced mechanisms for knowledge transfer between universities and industry is the consulting relationship. Typically a company contracts with a university faculty member to provide information or training in a specific area for a short period of time. The extent of corporate funding of such activities varies considerably within and across industries, as does the extent of faculty involvement across disciplines and universities (Brodsky, Kaufman, and Tooker, 1979).

A unique variation of this mechanism involving students is described by Hencke and others (1976). The program involved a visit by Yale graduate students to the Texaco Research Center at Beacon, New York. The visit included in-depth discussion of current research problems with Texaco staff and a tour of laboratory facilities. The six-person student team was then given three days to prepare a report of recommended actions, which was subsequently presented to Texaco staff for evaluation and feedback. The project lasted one week and each student consultant was paid a nominal fee.

The students apparently enjoyed the program and felt it provided a new experience in teamwork and increased their understanding of industry problems. Faculty, in turn, felt the program provided a rich addition to the basic graduate experience and an opening for future contacts with Texaco. Texaco received useful ideas and an opportunity to expose students to their needs, and staff received experience in research management.

There are some obvious limitations to consulting activities as a boundary-spanning structure. First of all, some schools formally restrict such activities, and faculty teaching or research commitments restrict this as a viable approach for others. In addition, there may be a value conflict for faculty opposed to research for profit. Finally, unless the individual consultant makes a conscious effort to share his or her experiences through lectures, publications, or informal discussions, others in the university will not profit from those experiences. However, it should be noted that some universities have brought consulting into the open, legitimated its existence, and been able to accrue significant benefits for their training and research efforts.

Continuing Education Programs. Continuing education activities are another category of university-industry exchange mechanisms. In general, continuing education includes those educational activities engaged in after full-time professional employment has begun and include courses that update one's knowledge in a current specialty or develop expertise in a new field. The mix of degree versus nondegree work varies, and two primary motives for support of or participation in continuing education are to improve employee current job performance or to prepare employees for increased responsibilities (Brodsky, Kaufman, and Tooker, 1979). Related to this are studies that show a positive relationship between company expenditures for R & D and continuing education and between participation in continuing education activities and staff R & D performance. Brodsky, Kaufman, and Tooker concluded from this information that continuing education "is considered a key factor in maintaining and stimulating vitality and innovation among engineers and scientists" (p. 71).

Current continuing education activities include courses tailored to individual company needs and the establishment of university programs on or near company locations. For example, in 1950 Syracuse University established an off-campus graduate program for IBM employees. Other innovations include television or videotaped courses, some of which allow audio interaction between students and instructors (Brodsky, Kaufman, and Tooker, 1979). There are, of course, a variety of sabbatical and scholarship programs for full-time study by industry staff.

As is the case with consulting arrangements, there are also barriers in both universities and companies to cooperation in continuing education activities, including academic disdain for faculty participation in noncredit or off-campus courses, and industry objections to higher education's emphasis on the theoretical rather than the practical and applied. For further information on employer/university interaction in the area of education and training, see Chapter Two, by Craig and Evers.

Rockwell International—An Innovative Ph.D. Program. There is a long history of industry involvement in university graduate training programs, such as internships, summer employment, fellowships. However, Rockwell International has established a program that is unique in its focus and scope (Cannon, 1980).

In 1976 Rockwell, through its corporate research laboratory, established a program at two predominantly black institutions to increase the number of minority Ph.D. engineers in the field of solid state electronics. The goals of the program encompassed both equity concerns and technological self-interest.

The company had reviewed the current numbers of new engineering Ph.D.s and realized that in 1977 out of approximately 44,000 less than 200 would be black. Rockwell realized it would be competing for about 100 minority graduates, only a few of whom would have expertise in solid state electronics. The company decided to deemphasize participation in a fruitless competitive recruitment effort and to take another tactic, to enlarge the future pool of talent thereby creating "a self-sustaining environment" (Cannon, 1980).

The program involved helping two black universities, Howard University and North Carolina Agricultural and Technical State University (A&T), to develop graduate programs in solid state electronics. Black institutions were chosen because 50 percent of all black engineers are trained in black colleges. The company transferred its process for producing gallium arsenide materials, which are used in lasers and light detectors, to these universities to help them establish research programs. The rationale was that a strong research program would attract both quality faculty and students. Rockwell also subcontracted research to the universities, supplied equipment, money, and the expertise to build the labs and organize the research programs. Additional financial support came from NASA and the Department of Energy (DOE). By early 1977, the equipment was in place and research programs were operational at both universities.

During the three years of program operations, Rockwell has contributed over $1 million, while NASA awarded grants to each university, and both schools are also participating in a $1 million DOE-sponsored joint university-industry solar cell research program managed by Rockwell.

These research projects helped to form the emerging graduate programs. Howard's Ph.D. program was established in the summer of 1980; North Carolina A&T is actively planning its program. Both programs have enrollments of approximately twelve students, half of whom are black, and several master's degrees are expected to be awarded this year. The addition of approximately three black Ph.D. engineers per year is admittedly small, but it represents a significant percentage increase in the existing pool. It is not suggested that a program of this scope could be easily duplicated, but the success of these activities does illustrate that small universities and large corporations can form mutually profitable relationships that stress both scientific and social objectives.

NSF Innovation Centers. In 1973 the National Science Foundation initiated a program to stimulate the development of entrepreneurial qualities in graduate students through formal training and hands-on experience. Three Innovation Centers were established—at M.I.T. Carnegie-Mellon, and the University of Oregon. (A fourth center was established at the University of Utah in 1977.) The three initial centers were provided a total of $3 million over a five-year period.

The unique features of these centers include the use of cooperative agreements as a funding device, rather than a grant or contract. This device allows NSF a more direct role in center activities, without rigidly defining the activities to be performed. Also of note are the centers' mandate to generate income and share in patents and inventions. All three centers combine coursework, clinical experience, research, and assistance to businesses. However, each center's structure and focus is somewhat different. One example is provided here.

The M.I.T. program is based in the engineering school and focuses on training in the innovation process itself. Students are offered five core courses in innovation and entrepreneurship, and direct exposure in a co-op program. This co-op program has three divisions: One is focused on the formation of student/faculty companies; in another, students and faculty develop products in response to specific industry requests; the other evaluates, develops, and licenses inventions to established businesses. In one year, the center received 139 "ideas" from nonstudents. However, priority was given to faculty and student work. To date, two companies have been formed. Products developed include a computer-controlled heating-air conditioning system, a TV tennis game, and a device to identify precious metals (Burger, 1979; Colton, Dec. 1979; Li and Jansson, 1979).

The center has had its problems. First, although it does not offer a degree program, some faculty saw the center as competing with more traditional programs for students. Second, co-op program activities were time-consuming and students often did not have sufficient knowledge or experience to develop products requested by industry. Third, the center itself was constrained from making quick decisions. Finally, students and faculty offered only a limited number and type of ideas for evaluation (Li and Jansson, 1979).

Plans are under way to alter the format of the center to compensate for these deficits. The new structure would include a center within the

School of Engineering and a development laboratory that would be financially separate from M.I.T., with faculty serving as consultants, and students as apprentices. Under this new format, the involvement of industry and the business community would be expanded and new faculty with expertise in innovation would be hired. Student involvement in the development of innovations would be tailored to their experience, interests, and time (Li and Jansson, 1979).

The continuation of this center after NSF funding ceased was partially based on its profits. As of 1978, over $500,000 in income was anticipated from royalties and contracts. M.I.T. also decided to include the center in its fund-raising activities (Burger, 1979).

The relative success of all three centers after six years of operation is impressive: More than 1,000 students have participated in over thirty new courses along with fifty-three faculty members and forty-six community associates. (It should be noted that although the schools were offering some courses prior to the establishment of the centers, the number of courses and students has increased.) A total of twenty-seven new products have been developed and twenty-nine new businesses started with total gross sales of $20 million in 1978. Approximately 800 new jobs will have been created (Colton, 1979). In addition, at least eight other schools are planning centers based on the NSF concept (Burger, 1979).

Harvard University—Genetic Engineering Company. A new type of university-industry linkage was recently considered and rejected by Harvard University. The faculty investigated the possibility of establishing a corporation to develop commercially promising faculty inventions in the area of genetic engineering.

The primary motivation for the plan was simple: money. The plan was seen as a way for the university to appropriate the benefits accruing from faculty work. Other benefits included facilitating technology transfer, that is, making research results available to the public more quickly (Hilts, 1980).

From an organizational perspective, the innovative aspect of the plan is that university research and industry application become linked within the larger umbrella organization of the university. Opponents of the plan raised the question of conflict of interest problems as well as the potential negative impact of these commercial activities on the structure, values, and reward systems of the university. A number of faculty agreed that "one of the most difficult problems in any joint venture between academe and industry would be the researcher's responsibility to disseminate information about research and the industrialist's desire to protect trade secrets." It was also pointed out that: "The university would have to be extremely careful not to let its financial interests influence its decisions about these topics, research proposals, admissions standards, or the employment and promotions of professors" (*Chronicle of Higher Education*, 1980a, p. 16).

Harvard faculty finally rejected the formation of this corporation because of "a number of potential conflicts with academic values" (*Chronicle of Higher Education*, 1980b, p. 1). According to Harvard President Derek Bok "the preservation of academic values is of paramount importance to the university" (*Chronicle of Higher Education*, 1980b, p. 1). However, Bok did not eliminate the possibility of university participation in such activities in the future, if the perceived value conflict could be resolved.

Conclusion

Our approach has been to avoid prescriptive and normative statements and to lay out an array of operational options. In this closing section, we would like to highlight some of the unresolved issues that cut across all our previous narrative.

As previously discussed, the current driving force behind much of the federal funding for university-industry initiatives lies in the concerns about manufacturing productivity and technological innovation. Many of the exchange options just discussed are based on the premise of external federal support. In evaluating their relative worth, readers should be advised that federal support in the future cannot be predicted on the basis of support in the past.

Aside from the potential for changing funding priorities already noted, there are a number of federal policy levers that have an impact on university-industry activities. For example, there is currently no uniform government-wide policy regarding patent rights for inventions resulting from federally sponsored R&D. Tax and investment policies also can have a potentially negative impact on university-industry relations by discouraging investment in equipment and reducing corporate equity used to finance long-term research. However, the case studies have illustrated that creative, mutually satisfying solutions can be worked out even under current policies.

Health, environmental, and safety regulations have reduced university-industry incentives for linkages in four ways: through shifts in the allocation of resources (from research to mandated plant and equipment revisions); by increasing the waiting time on returns for investments (mandatory testing of drugs); through restrictions on areas of research (genetic engineering); and by increasing uncertainty (the probability of regulatory changes complicates long-term planning and investment of funds).

A special category of regulations includes antitrust laws, which can discourage or prohibit cooperative industry ventures in support of university research. The need for cooperation between firms has, of course, intensified as the costs of supporting large-scale research efforts have expanded. Whether specific changes in the laws are needed is unclear. It has been suggested that a clarification of policy would in itself facilitate cooperative research activities. The government has agreed to provide this needed clarification (Prager and Omenn, 1980).

Finally, grant and contract reporting requirements can pose a specific barrier to university participation in federally funded cooperative research activities. The most controversial provision, OMB Circular AO-21, mandates 100 percent time and effort reporting by researchers on federal grants. These requirements were instituted to monitor the rapid increase in university indirect cost rates on research projects.

The combined effect of these policy levels has been to increase the risk or uncertainty of corporate investment in long-term research, which is a primary activity in universities. The choice of specific options to reduce this uncertainty is dependent, in part, on the extent of government involvement in encouraging these linkages. A spectrum of roles has been suggested ranging from no interference to equal partnership with both sectors, depending on the federal objective to be realized.

Thus, if the government's primary objective is to facilitate industry participation, tax and investment incentives and revised patent policies could suffice. If the objective is to facilitate university participation, then changes in accountability mechanisms should be considered. A still more direct role would involve funding of cooperative projects. A basic question is the degree, and longevity of commitment by university and industry to promoting collaborative interaction. Answering this question is perhaps even more crucial for university actors. As Drucker has noted, "Science . . . has a greater stake in the survival of an autonomous and self-governing industry than industry has in the survival of an autonomous and self-governing science" (1979, p. 810). We hope that this chapter will provide some impetus for university administrators to consider that balance and the options presented here.

References

Abernathy, W., and Utterback, J. M. "Patterns of Industrial Innovation." *Technology Review*, June/July 1978, pp. 41–47.

Allen, T. J. *Managing the Flow of Technology*. Cambridge, Mass: M.I.T. Press, 1977.

Baer, W. S. *Strenthening University-Industry Interactions*. Santa Monica, Calif.: RAND Corporation, Jan. 1980.

Battelle Memorial Institute. *Interactions of Science and Technology in the Innovation Process: Some Case Studies*. Final Report to the National Science Foundation NSF–C667. Columbus, Ohio: Battelle Memorial Institute, 1973.

Birch D. "The Job Generation Process." Unpublished manuscript. Cambridge, Mass.: Program on Neighborhood and Regional Change, M.I.T., 1979.

Brodsky, N., Kaufman, H. G., and Tooker, J. D. *University Industry Cooperation:*

A Preliminary Analysis of Existing Mechanisms and Their Relationship to the Innovation Process. New York: New York University Center for Science and Technology Policy, July 1979.

Brown, G. E. "University-Industry Links: Government as Blacksmith." Paper presented at AAAS Symposium on Government/Industry/University Relations, San Francisco, Jan. 5, 1980.

Burger, R. M. *An Analysis of the National Science Foundation's Innovation Centers Experiment.* North Carolina: Research Triangle Institute, July 1979.

Bush, V. *Science: The Endless Frontier.* Washington, D.C.: U.S. Government Printing Office, July 1945.

Cannon, P. "University Minority Doctoral Engineering Programs." *Research Management,* 1980, *13* (1), 21–23.

Colton, R. M. "Innovation Center: A Future Dimension in Engineering Education." *American Society of Mechanical Engineers Proceedings,* Winter annual meeting, Dec. 1979.

Cordes, J. J. *The Impact of Tax and Financial Regulatory Policies on Industrial Innovation.* Washington, D.C.: National Academy of Sciences, 1980.

Drucker, P. F. "Science and Industry: Challenges of Antagonistic Interdependence." *Science,* 1979, *204* (4395), 806–810.

Gellman Research Associates, Inc. "Indicators of International Trends in Technological Innovation." *Science Indicators 1976.* Washington, D.C.: National Science Board, 1977.

Goldblith, S. A. Testimony before the U.S. House of Representatives, Committee on Science and Technology Subcommittee on Science and Technology, July 31, August 1, 2, 1979. *Hearings on Government and Innovation: University-Industry Taxations.* Washington, D.C.: U.S. Government Printing Office, 1979, pp. 285–335.

"Harvard Abandons Plan for Role in Genetic Engineering Company." *Chronicle of Higher Education,* Nov. 24, 1980b, pp. 1, 4.

"Harvard Weighs Setting Up Company to Run Genetic Engineering Business." *Chronicle of Higher Education,* Nov. 3, 1980a, pp. 1, 16.

Hencke, W. R., and others. "A Program for Student Involvement in Industrial R&D." *Research Management,* 1976, *1261,* 32–34.

Hilts, P. J. "Ivy-Covered Capitalism." *Washington Post,* November 10, 1980, pp. A-1, A-30, A-32.

ITT Research Institute. *Technology in Retrospect and Critical Events in Science.* Report to the National Science Foundation, ITT Research Institute, 1968.

Levine, S., and White, P. "Exchange as a Conceptual Framework for the Study of Interorganizational Relationships." *Administrative Science Quarterly.* 1961, *5,* 583–601.

Li, Y. T., and Jansson, D. "Specific Case Studies-Innovation Center." In N. S. Kapany (Ed.), *Innovation Entrepreneurship and the University.* Santa Cruz, Calif.: Center for Innovation and Entrepreneurial Development, 1979.

Mogee, M. E. "The Relationship of Federal Support of Basic Research in Universities to Industrial Innovation and Productivity." Washington, D.C.: Congressional Research Service, Library of Congress, Aug. 24, 1979.

National Science Foundation. "Research and Development and Economic Progress." *Science and Technology: Annual Report to the Congress.* Washington, D.C.: National Science Foundation, Aug. 1978.

National Science Foundation and the Department of Education. *Science and Engineering Education for the 1980s and Beyond.* Washington, D.C.: National Science Foundation and the Department of Education, 1980.

Prager, D. J., and Omenn, G. S. "Research, Innovation, and University Industry Linkages." *Science,* 1980, *20F* (4429), 379–384.

Reid, W. J. "Interorganizational Coordination in Social Welfare: A Theoretical Approach to Analysis and Intervention." In R. M. Kramer and H. Specht (Eds.), *Readings in Community Organization Practice.* Englewood Cliffs, N.J.: Prentice-Hall, 1969.

Shapero, A. *University-Industry Interactions: Recurring Expectations, Unwarranted Assumptions, and Feasible Policies.* Columbus: Ohio State University, 1979.

Sherwin, E. W., and Isenson, R. S. "Project Hindsight." *Science,* 1967, *156,* 1571–1577.

Souder, W. E. "An Exploratory Study of the Coordinating Mechanisms between R & D and Marketing as an Influence on the Innovation Process." Final Report to the National Science Foundation. Pittsburgh, Pa.: University of Pittsburgh, 1978.

Tornatzky, L., and others. *Innovation and Social Process.* Elmsford, N.Y.: Pergamon Press, 1980.

Tornatzky, L., and Lounsbury, J. W. "Dimensions of Interorganizational Interaction in Social Agencies." *Journal of Community Psychology,* 1979, *7,* 198–209.

Elmima C. Johnson is a policy analyst, Division of Industrial Science and Technological Innovation, National Science Foundation. Previously she served in various administrative positions in the Department of Education including special assistant to the assistant secretary for post secondary education. She has also held teaching positions at several universities, including Michigan State University, where she received her Ph.D.

Louis G. Tornatzky is head of the section on Innovation Processes Research, Division of Industrial Science and Technological Innovation, National Science Foundation. Prior to this, he was professor of urban and metropolitan studies and psychology at Michigan State University.

*The individual's ability to function effectively in
society differs from the ability to observe and
understand society and its work roles. Which
responsibilities for training are appropriate to higher
education and which to employers?*

Colleges, Universities, and Corporate Training

Ernest A. Lynton

To apply John Dunlop's term the "shadow educational system" (Weeks,
1975) to corporate training and development activities is both significant
and misleading. It implies, correctly, that many corporate programs are
quite similar to what is done in educational institutions. Yet it suggests, er-
roneously, a conscious attempt to duplicate the existing educational system.

Corporate instruction differs from traditional schooling in strategy,
often in structure, and usually in the system for access. Educational institutions could under no circumstances assume the full responsibility for all
corporate training needs, just as corporations could not deal with the
general broad educational and cultural development of adults. The question, rather, is whether it is possible and desirable to increase the present
limited extent to which some of the corporate human resource needs are
met by colleges and universities.

This chapter will pursue that question with regard to the
continuing developmental needs of employees, but some attention will

The research on which this paper is based was supported by the Ford
Foundation.

G. Gold (Ed.), *New Directions for Experiential Learning: Business and Higher Education—
Towards New Alliances*, no. 13. San Francisco: Jossey-Bass, September 1981.

65

also be paid to the education of individuals before they are employed. Two basic questions are common to both:

1. Does the responsibility of colleges and universities for individual development go beyond cognitive and intellectual formation to include more emphasis on the ability to function effectively on the job and in society?

2. Would corporate goals be better met if training and development went beyond specific task-oriented skills to include more emphasis on individuals' ability to think about and to understand their tasks and the environment in which they operate?

The premise of the chapter is that both questions have an affirmative answer. More linkage between the two sectors will enhance the ability of each to meet these broader goals. On the basis of an analysis of the different perspectives held by each side, this chapter proposes a set of issues that must be dealt with if these links are to be forged in a meaningful way.

The Corporate View of the Academy

The business community at all levels is pervasively critical of the academy, with much justification. The criticisms fall into three broad categories.

Pedagogical Issues. Most employers complain that graduates of colleges and universities are simply not prepared to be effective members of an organization.

In the first place, many students obtain baccalaureate and even graduate degrees with inadequate basic skills, particularly in the area of communication. Many of them write badly, speak badly, and listen badly— all serious handicaps to the necessary relationships in a complex organization.

In addition, employers view academic curricula as too narrowly focused on cognitive content, with inadequate attention to behavioral and affective factors. Equally serious is the related accusation that colleges and universities are too theoretical and too abstract, with inadequate inclusion of practical experiences and with too few faculty members who have themselves had periods of activity "in the real world." Students by and large are seen as inadequately prepared to analyze and deal with complex situations and to work as part of a problem-solving team.

All of this adds up to a pervasive feeling that academic institutions provide inadequate preparation for the transition from theory to practice, and that even technically well-prepared graduates are not employable without further training. Companies are forced to provide what from their point of view constitutes remedial instruction in interpersonal skills. Given this dissatisfaction with the preparation of college graduates, it is little wonder that the corporate sector is reluctant to turn to the academy for much involvement in further human resource development. If this is to be changed, higher education must clearly accept much greater and more explicit responsibility for preparing individuals to function effectively on the job.

Related to this corporate criticism is the widespread view that most faculty members simply do not know how to teach adults, especially those who return to the classroom with a great deal of prior work experience. As corporations themselves gain more extensive experience in training adults, their criticism of higher education becomes more pointed and more self-confident.

Attitudinal Issues. Most outside observers agree on one fundamental point: Academic institutions must learn to work together with industry and other external clients in defining educational needs and developing appropriate content and format. Unwillingness to do this is viewed, quite simply, as arrogance and constitutes one of the major barriers to effective linkages. In a recent address to the American Association of Higher Education, Cross (1981) gave a number of examples of categories of cooperative efforts, bringing out some of the problems and limitations of each. She added: "Higher education has much to learn about being a good partner. Reducing potential industrial partners to the status of junior partners whose task it is to offer support without criticism is not likely to result in a constructive or lasting relationship. Neither is selling our soul for a mess of short-range benefits. But establishing partnerships based on mutual trust and respect and a careful consideration of what each has to offer is a pathway that seems clearly indicated on the new frontier."

The attitudes and insights of the adult learners themselves is a second issue to which little attention has been paid to date. In making instructional arrangements with a corporate client, the academic institution enters into a trilateral relationship in which the individual student constitutes the third party. Part of the challenge of teaching adult and experienced individuals is that their views and reactions as to content and format must be taken seriously and that they must be used as "evaluators of their educational experience" (Cross, 1981).

Organizational and Administrative Issues. The instructional needs of the corporate world are manifold and must be met by a variety of program formats, from occasional seminars to multiweek, fully residential programs. If academic institutions are to provide even a fraction of this broad array, they must develop more flexible and responsive administrative policies and procedures. With regard to program design, review, and approval, colleges and universities must find a middle ground between the traditional lengthy process and some "rubber stamp" procedure that eliminates the benefits of academic oversight.

Admissions and registration procedures must be streamlined and made more flexible. The apparent dilemma between the corporate desire to have a program open to all employees and the institutional insistence on degree standards can be resolved quite easily by distinguishing between admission to a course and admission to degree candidacy. The latter can be made conditional on the successful completion of a few courses.

Adaptability of time, place, and format of instructional programs is of the utmost importance if higher education is to increase its service to the corporate sector. In this as in the area of program content, academic institutions need to sit down with potential industrial clients to work out the details. For example, it may be necessary to examine the relative advantages of the convenience of on-site instruction with the countervailing advantages of an on-campus program with access to libraries and with mixing of students from different backgrounds. A number of corporations and unions have found that their employees prefer the latter in spite of considerable additional cost and time for travel.

Flexible ways must also be found to make faculty available for a variety of instructional tasks in increments of time less than the full course for a whole semester. If colleges and universities do not provide this possibility through an institutional mechanism, the corporate sector will continue to engage faculty on an individual basis as consultants. This practice is very prevalent, with corporations employing many faculty members as designers and instructors, either on a direct consulting basis or as consultants to the external training agencies. In this way, a corporation or a consulting firm obtains the services of a faculty member at marginal cost, without having to pay the indirect, overhead costs of the institution that furnishes the individual with a basic salary, office and research facilities, health insurance, and other fringe benefits. Educational institutions should try to find mechanisms, such as the practice plans existing in medical schools, through which they are compensated for these indirect expenses.

Taken together, these three categories of necessary changes in the academy—pedagogy, attitude, and organization and administration—constitute a powerful agenda for discussion and problem solving between business and higher education. A combination of sophistication, sensitivity, diplomacy, and tough-skinned determination will be required of higher education leaders seeking to pursue these issues with corporations.

An Academic's View of Corporate Education

The academic observer finds much to question in corporate training practices. The least expected characteristic of employer-sponsored corporate training and development is the pervasive emphasis on interpersonal relationships, human behavior, teamwork, and organizational development. To a considerable extent, this is a response to the increase in organizational complexity within companies even of moderate size. More and more of them are becoming "matrix organizations" (Janger, 1979) with flexible patterns for horizontal as well as vertical relationships and communication in which responsibility is not always accompanied by authority. This demands considerable social as well as technical sophistication from all participants in order to maintain organizational effectiveness.

The search for effective designs for management flexibility, control, and communication is one of the principal forces shaping corporate training and development today. An important component of all this is an emphasis, as well, on job satisfaction as a contributor both to productivity and the quality of work life (Bentley and Hansen, 1980). All of this has led to a strong, perhaps excessive emphasis on behavioral and affective factors.

The second major characteristic of the majority of corporate programs is their narrow definition: They are usually relevant to a particular task or an immediate set of circumstances and have a well-defined and limited range of use. As a result within the span from "education" to "training" suggested by Branscomb and Gilmore (1975), most of corporate human resource development is at the training end. This is understandable and, on the whole, appropriate to the purposes and priorities of the corporate sector. All expenditures of time and money must be justified in terms of the ultimate goal of profitability, toward which training and development are only the means. The orientation of American industry toward short-term payoff has not been conducive to long-range developmental activities.

However, one can argue that the long-term effectiveness and profitability of business and industry requires a reexamination of this fundamental issue. The current reliance on skill training derived from specific and immediate task analyses is based, implicitly, on three premises: (1) little or no change is anticipated in the basic theories and concepts that employees presumably acquired during their formative education; (2) employers expect a continuing ability to hire new employees more recently educated if substantial conceptual and methodological changes do occur; and (3) only a relatively small group of employees needs to have a basic understanding of the background and the concepts underlying corporate activities.

The first of these assumptions is patently incorrect. The content of an academic degree in almost any discipline today is substantially different from what it was a decade ago. The second premise raises the crucial issue of employee stability. Increasingly, employers in the private sector perceive—whether as a positive development or as an unavoidable liability is not clear—a growth in stability and permanence of their labor force (*Engineering News*, 1979). This is reflected in the change from the title of personnel directors to human resource managers. This implies that the work force constitutes a long-term investment that needs to be maintained, refurbished, and renovated as much as a company's physical resources.

The third implicit premise appears to be contrary to the growing organizational complexity: the need for multiple interactions and the growing emphasis on job satisfaction through participation in decision making.

A reexamination of the three assumptions, therefore, may make it increasingly important to ensure ongoing renewal of the theoretical foundations and basic understanding with which employees apply their basic skills. Managerial and professional employees should be able to update their academic degrees on a periodic basis, not only refreshing their understanding of the original content, but also learning the new material that was included in the curriculum since their graduation. Theoretical concepts and basic insights change with time, and keeping pace with this is important to any individual's ongoing intellectual vitality, which in turn affects job effectiveness. The more this becomes an operational principle, the greater will be the interest and willingness of private employers to invest in long-range intellectual and human development in addition to task-oriented training.

The need for this is evident for those who are rising on the hierarchical ladder, but it is equally important for those who will not move into the narrow apex of the corporate pyramid and remain, instead, at a middle-management level. Their continuing effectiveness at the plateau that they have reached should be of particular importance to all employers, but it would appear that their needs have only to a minor extent been considered in the design of corporate education and training. The importance of this issue is again clearly related to employee stability.

An outside observer is struck by the extent to which corporate discussion of these issues has been professionalized into a distinct vocation of human resource and organizational development, with its own national associations, publications, meetings and, inevitably, its own jargon. This has many advantages, in that it serves to create a network of information and of exchange of experience, as well as to translate basic theoretical concepts into practical terms and applicable programs. But there exists, as well, the danger that a profession becomes a closed circle, in which corporate staff and external consultants reinforce each other without much disinterested critique, and through which valid concepts may degenerate into catch phrases and simplistic mnemonics. To the extent to which such a danger exists, it is reinforced by the scarcity of evaluations of corporate training and development (Woodlington, 1980).

The criteria for such evaluations must of necessity be the extent to which the programs meet the goals of corporate improvement and profitability, not whether they benefit the individual. If there is to be closer collaboration between the corporate world and the academy in the design and implementation of instructional programs, the academic participants must realize the inevitable and quite appropriate distinction between the basic objectives of the two disparate sectors. In corporate training and development, program content is designed and participants are selected on the basis of the needs and the priorities of the employer rather than in terms of the optimal development of the individual.

In most cases, employees are identified for successive stages of development at some time while they are at the preceding managerial level. Some of the largest companies, however, have in recent years instituted more of a long-range developmental approach to ensure the availability of properly trained candidates for top executive positions ten and twenty years later. In such a "successor planning system," as it is formally called in one large corporation, strategic planning includes estimates of future needs at senior executive levels. This leads to the identification, at a very junior level, of their career in the company, of about three times the ultimately needed number of highly promising young managers. These individuals follow a sophisticated and elaborate plan for development, which combines successive periods of training and education with a series of appointments in different segments of the corporation.

Conclusion

Clearly there are substantial barriers to enlarging the role of colleges and universities in corporate training and development. The educational and the business sectors must of necessity pursue very distinct goals with quite different priorities. The ultimate purpose of the former, which is the development of the individual, is merely a means to the ends of productivity and profitability for the latter. That is inherent in the two systems and not subject to change.

However, it would appear to be of mutual benefit to try and modify policies, procedures, and attitudes in both sectors. Colleges and universities are likely to become better institutions and make more progress toward their own objectives if they accept more responsibility for the preparation of individuals to function effectively in society. Corporations are likely to enhance their strength and ability to deal with changing circumstances by placing more emphasis on continuing intellectual vitality and an updating of conceptual foundations as part of their human resource development.

In essence, this will require a determined effort of both sides to reduce the present gap between the worlds of learning and of work and to lessen the separation between education and training.

References

Bentley, M. T., and Hansen, G. B. "Improving Productivity via QWL Centers." *Training and Development Journal*, 1980, *34* (30), 30–35.

Branscomb, L. M., and Gilmore, P. C. "Education in Private Industry." *Daedalus,* Winter 1975, pp. 222–233.

Cross, K. P. "Exploring New Frontiers in Higher Education." Delta Epsilon Sigma Lecture presented at the National Conference on Higher Education, AAHE,

72

Washington, D.C., March 1981, *Current Issues in Higher Education, 1981* (forthcoming).

Janger, A. R. *Matrix Organization in Complex Businesses.* Report No. 763. New York: The Conference Board, 1979.

"Stable Employment: A $5.7 Billion Saving." *Engineering News*, 1979, *202* (58).

Weeks, D. A. (Ed.). *Human Resources: Toward Rational Policy.* Report No. 669. New York: The Conference Board, 1975.

Woodlington, D. "Some Impressions of the Evaluation of Training in Industry." *Phi Delta Kappan*, Jan. 1980, pp. 326–328.

Ernest A. Lynton is now Commonwealth Professor of the University of Massachusetts after fifteen years in academic administration. He was founding dean of Livingston College at Rutgers University, then academic vice president for the University of Massachusetts.

*What are the benefits of cross-sector programs to
learners? Substantial and diverse incentives for
learning are built into employer–higher
education programs.*

Incentives for Learning and Innovation

Lynn A. DeMeester

One of the most important questions to ask about higher education-business programs is: What is the benefit of these activities to the learner? If educators and employers operate on the assumption that learning can occur in a variety of settings for different purposes, higher education-business collaboration can have enormous potential for extending the resources of both the college and the employer and, more importantly, for creating new opportunities for learners.

Almost all young people and many adults have little work experience and even less knowledge of how to advance their careers in this complex society. Young people in high school and college, high school dropouts, high school graduates who have "bounced around" in postdiploma uncertainty, young adults leaving the military, women seeking part-time or full-time employment after years out of the labor market, older workers displaced by technology, urban residents who come to higher education seeking to move themselves out of a rut—all lack the kinds of work experiences that are attractive to employers. All have the potential to be victims of a fragmented work structure that leaves some unemployed, many with jobs, but few with a meaningful career. When most learners come to college, therefore, they need more than a process of gathering knowledge for its own sake; they need to build credibility, to explore

G. Gold (Ed.), *New Directions for Experiential Learning: Business and Higher Education—Towards New Alliances*, no. 13. San Francisco: Jossey-Bass, September 1981.

aptitudes and career interests, and to acquire new skills and knowledge that employers will value. They need the opportunity, through work and service experiences, to systematically explore the tasks, roles, problems, and rewards of working in real-world institutions. These needs put a heavy burden on higher education to assure that the time and effort learners spend do contribute both to learners personally and to their value to prospective employers.

Higher education–business relationships can benefit learners in other ways as well. For example, work experience may be part of a learner's financial aid package, or even the only source of income support. Other support services such as job placement, career counseling, child care, scheduling, transportation, housing, tutoring and mentoring, and health insurance may all be affected by higher education–business relationships or their absence. Indirect financial assistance of which learners are often unaware may also come through corporate philanthropy to the institution, enabling the institution to hold down tuition costs. The potential benefits to learners, in sum, are complex and frequently, as with the political support provided by business membership on college boards of trustees, beyond the horizons visible to most students.

Another fundamental question regarding higher education–business initiatives should be: What is the benefit to the faculty? To many educators, the benefits of working with employers appear obvious. For those faculty who enjoy making off-campus contacts, setting up internships, teaching employers how to use work as a learning experience for students, and working with returning adults who have been full-time employees, the rewards are intrinsic. Rewards may also be obvious to a professor who sees corporate investment in on-campus basic research as a means to upgrade laboratory equipment, conduct more expensive experiments, hire more graduate assistants, write more papers, receive more recognition from colleagues, and develop consulting opportunities.

For other faculty, the benefits may be less clear. In an environment of enrollment declines or even steady state, the growth of joint programs between colleges and businesses can appear to threaten already existing programs within departments. The appropriateness of granting degree credit for off-campus field experience or for learning from work and life experience may be questioned, since faculty may perceive these as substituting experience for classroom learning. Even if the learning from these experiences is documented or if an antecedent course has been developed to provide preparation for analyzing field experience, some faculty may view these programs as a threat to academic standards or to the integrity of the on-campus curriculum.

A key concern for all faculty is whether institutional rewards are attainable through participation in such activities. Administrators may applaud community projects but fail to provide release time, clerical support, or clear the procedural and scheduling questions inevitably raised by registrars and department chairpersons. Faculty may be forced to treat off-campus projects or assessment of learning from life and work experience as labors of love rather than routine, legitimate responsibilities. Participation in cooperative education, internship projects, field research programs, and lifelong learning programs may not enhance faculty portfolios for promotion and tenure decisions. The most powerful factor in achieving faculty involvement and support, therefore, is top-level leadership that makes relationships with employers and other community agencies central to the mission, operating procedures, and reward structure of a college or university.

Since its formation under the Education Amendments Act of 1972, the Fund for the Improvement of Postsecondary Education (FIPSE) has sought to encourage and nurture innovative projects benefiting learners and faculty. FIPSE has used a foundation-like "seed money" approach to solicit creative ideas that will move institutions toward fundamental, permanent improvement in the ways they provide equal educational opportunities. Among the innovative projects supported by the fund have been many involving higher education–business collaboration.

The fund's legislative charter is broad yet specific. "Improved educational opportunities" are seen as related to technology, structural changes within institutions, cost-effectiveness of educational programs, improving accessibility of postsecondary education to learners, improved graduate and professional education, credentialing functions, development of new institutions and programs stressing experiential learning, and the overall promotion of innovation and equal opportunity (Education Amendments Act of 1972). Thus, in an eight-year history of supporting nearly 700 projects across the nation the fund has been able to encourage creative action in almost every aspect of the postsecondary teaching/learning process.

At every step, FIPSE staff have been keenly aware of the roles of relevant parties in addition to students and faculty. What is the benefit of a project to postsecondary administrators and their institutions? What benefits and costs accrue to businessperson, workplace supervisor, labor union leader and members? Realistic responses to the questions of "who benefits" must precede any decision to support a proposed project.

Consequently, one of the fund's greatest opportunities to emphasize quality is at the inception of a project. The fund examines the applicant's track record, advanced planning, and prospects for project continuation. Good ideas are essential. But good ideas will not go far without a carefully designed project strategy. Commitments must be lined up beforehand, both within and outside the college. If the concept is exceptionally creative, FIPSE may risk the chance that some commitments will be "nailed down" as the project proceeds. However, the best proof of commitment is that the idea being presented has already been tested on a small scale and already been approved in concept and even in practice by internal administrators and faculty. Where contacts with business are involved, viable working relationships are essential.

The aim of this chapter is to explore how these pieces—learners, faculty, administrators, employers, and institutions—fall into place to create exciting learning opportunities. For a number of reasons, the focus is on employer roles, especially private-sector employers. First, the crisis of higher education today is at one level a crisis of demographics. Employers through their hiring, training, work, and retirement practices exert a major influence on the size and profile of the total population available as college enrollments.

Second, the fund is concerned with the quality and accessibility of postsecondary learning wherever it takes place. The workplace is increasingly available as a setting for formal as well as informal learning. The fund is interested in genuine responses to the needs and unique situations of working adults, who increasingly want career information, career planning skills, and specific skills and knowledge.

Third, connections between work and education largely ignored during 1960s must be developed more systematically if higher education institutions are to define their value and place in American society over the next decade and beyond. The fund's small but visible efforts are intended to help creative leaders at the institutional level design exploratory relationships that may point the way to a new equilibrium between education and work.

This chapter uses examples from many of the projects supported by the fund to show how collaborative higher education–business activities can be linked to incentives that motivate adult learners. These examples fall into five categories of incentives: developing new knowledge and skills; making a positive contribution to communities; removing scheduling, location, and financial barriers; improving access to postprogram employment; and improving internal higher education–business procedures and service delivery. As will be evident, most of these and other fund projects provide multiple incentives and, by emphasizing specific aspects, could be used as examples in several categories. The examples are selected from FIPSE projects described in annual editions of *Resources for Change: A Guide to Projects* (for example, Fund for Improvement in Postsecondary Education, 1980, 1981).

New Knowledge and Skills

The American Management Association (AMA) became concerned that mid-level managers lacked opportunities and programs to prepare them for future responsibilities. The AMA is attempting to overcome deficiencies of existing graduate management programs. The AMA Manager Competency Model, the result of five years of research on 2,000 managers, identifies eighteen generic skills competencies closely related to superior job performance in private-sector mid-level management positions. The result of the programs is a Master of Management degree program available to AMA members and, eventually, other institutions and businesses. This project exemplifies that a program developed in the business sector can potentially serve as a model to postsecondary institutions.

A project sponsored by the New York City Police Foundation, a private nonprofit organization, seeks to improve the writing skills that are fundamental to police work. In cooperation with John Jay College of Criminal Justice, the New York City Police are analyzing a variety of documents produced in police work. As a result of the analysis, a pilot program to improve writing is under way for detectives, sergeants, and lieutenants. Faculty from John Jay College assist with the document analysis and curriculum development.

The Artists Foundation (Boston) serves in a "brokering" capacity by teaching individual and performing artists professional management skills necessary to operate a small business as one career option. The foundation's curriculum is also being tested for use in college art departments and schools.

Another project defines professional competencies that help workers become managers of their small industries. The Industrial Cooperative Association (ICA), a nonprofit organization founded in 1977, is developing an adult education program for workers who organize worker-owned cooperatives. The program serves over 100 workers in several national sites and concentrates on the management and decision-making skills that workers need as they assume administrative as well as production duties. Like the AMA project, this project results from a grass-roots initiative by the employer organization. One of the interesting results of the AMA and ICA projects will be their applicability to and impact upon curricula offered by higher education institutions.

Learner Contributions to Their Communities

At Stanford University, faculty, students, agencies, and businesses work together on community action projects. The program, started by students in the early 1970s, has been incorporated into the university's permanent curriculum. About 150 students work each year on projects at public agencies and businesses. Project administrators serve as a "broker" between employers, students, and faculty. The employers identify critical problems facing their organizations. Back on campus, the project staff form teams of students and faculty who can provide help. Faculty members are selected on the basis of their academic expertise and ability to act as mentors for students in a real-world consulting situation during the semester-long project. Students participate based upon their academic studies. Unlike many experiential learning projects, faculty members, students, and employers form a team to work toward the solution of community-defined problems. The teams have worked on problems in areas such as transportation, conservation, minority rights, criminal justice, and education.

Another approach to community service is under way at the University of Southern California (USC). USC's Joint Educational Project started in 1972 as an attempt to assist the low-income, minority community. The project involves a network of over 4,000 parents, teachers, and students by linking undergraduate students as volunteers with existing service projects in community schools and health agencies. Through semester-long projects, students combine service to the community with experience that relates to their studies. In 1977, 1,000 students (10 percent of USC's undergraduate population) participated in projects in over fifty public and private agencies.

At the University of Pittsburgh, twenty-five M.B.A. students a year participate in a semester-long consulting project in the minority business community of Pittsburgh. Students spend one semester on the theoretical aspects of small business, one semester in the internship, and a follow-up semester to help students apply their experience to business principles. As a result of this program, the university realized that its business curricula needed to be enriched with examples of problems and management issues unique to small business enterprises. Most texts available for M.B.A. programs emphasize the operations of large corporations. Developed with business leaders, a number of curriculum modules are now a part of the graduate curriculum. In addition, the university conducts monthly workshops for the business community on such topics as taxation and labor management. Part of the impetus for the program originated from the isolation that had developed between the urban institutions and the minority business community. The project creates new bridges with the community while simultaneously realizing educational benefits for students.

Removing Scheduling, Location, and Financial Barriers

A number of projects nationally sponsored by higher education institutions aid women who are returning to college. A two-year project (1977–1979) at the University of Kentucky (Lexington) developed a paid internship in the private sector to help women returning to college pursue their degree. The internship carried academic credit and simultaneously enabled women to build a portfolio of experience while completing academic work. Although some businesses balked initially at the payment feature, employers requested new interns. Several employers experimented with approaches for sponsoring the women, "mentoring with an administrator." One of the difficulties all employers express is integrating the short-term nature of the internship into the ongoing workflow of the organization.

Other projects supported by the fund have attempted to serve the needs of working women trapped in low-paying jobs. The National Council of Negro Women (NCNW) worked with Pace University (New York City) to develop a sixty credit A.A. program for minority women in clerical positions who lacked career opportunities to advance. During the three-year grant, NCNW served over 155 women in thirty-five companies. NCNW provided counseling services for the women and negotiated with employers for educational benefits and job advancements for the participants. In addition, NCNW attempted to design with Pace University a program that would prepare the women for sales and other mid-level positions. In this project, as in several others the fund has supported, a third-party "broker" serves a constituency by bringing together educational and business resources.

In a similar example, from 1977 to 1980 the National Institute for Work and Learning's (NIWL) Center for Women and Work provided career counseling services and seminars to over 3,700 clerical women through working women's organizations located in six cities across the country.

A project to help another group of women is being undertaken by Smith College. Smith is inaugurating a program to help corporate women to break through mid-management into top-management positions. At the inception of the project, its director contacted employers (often through the alumnae network) by letter and telephone, followed by a visit. In the fall of 1980, the project director visited nearly 100 of the Fortune 500 companies in preparation for sponsoring two summer workshops for the women with an intervening year project at the corporate site. Corporations agree to sponsor a participant, pay all fees, maintain all benefits, and send the participant's manager to a two-day workshop.

At the University of San Francisco, as a result of inquiries from business people, an alternative approach developed to provide technical assistance to the Asian business community. The university combines computerized instruction and video cassettes to offer thirty modules of instruction to business people at two secondary schools located in the community. The modular curriculum provides a means to reach workers at times and places that are convenient to the working schedules of small business managers.

Improving Access to Postprogram Employment

A project at Snow College (Ephraim, Utah) provides a fifteen-week program to prepare youth for either a job or entry into an academic program. The project director personally visited over 800 employers in the fall of 1979 and secured several hundred job slots for youth. Positions were located in auto repair, construction, and food service organizations. These contacts are tremendously important in sustaining a "base" of placements for future as well as currently enrolled students. One hypothesis explaining the success of the college in securing job placements is that higher education institutions command a respect in the business community that results in employment opportunities not normally made available for CETA youth. Employers reported that their involvement resulted in a new, positive perception of CETA workers.

Other projects also work toward promoting equity by affording students opportunities to demonstrate the value of their work to employers who might have been reluctant to hire them otherwise. At Kansas City Community College, fifty handicapped and disabled students pursue individualized career preparation programs. The college helps the students and employers prepare for the experience. A labor-industry council helps prepare employers for employing students. The work experience component enables employers to see that handicapped individuals can serve as productive employees and simultaneously employers are able to refer handicapped individuals to the college.

Northeastern University (Boston) developed a fifteen-month career reentry program for women in collaboration with twelve major corporations in Boston. The program attempted to build upon the skills and interests that women often acquire through community and volunteer activities. Employers such as the Polaroid Corporation identified mid-level jobs with advancement potential that they could promise to women who completed the program. The Northeastern administrators and employers identified competencies required for each job. Northeastern selected twenty-four women (from over 400 applicants) and also conducted a core management seminar followed by an individualized one-year program for the women. Employers supervised the women in an internship. At the completion of the pilot program, women moved into mid-level positions in the corporate sector. For the women, the short-term program provided an alternative to the time-consuming prospect of earning a four-year degree. Employers were able to specify competencies requisite for career positions and the institution was able to provide a viable educational alternative to women returning to college.

Faculty at Northeast Illinois University who recognized the serious shortages of secondary and elementary school teaching positions reexamined the basic assumptions of the teacher training curriculum. Believing that teaching is relevant to a number of career fields, faculty designed an internship program in nonschool settings. During 1981–1982, approximately 140 education undergraduates will work in twenty-five businesses, industries, and social service agencies.

Some projects are overcoming barriers of socialization and attitude by directing women into nontraditional careers they might not have considered ten years ago. At Keller Graduate School (Chicago), a project helps the generalist B.A. woman broaden her career options through a summer program that includes an orientation course and a ten-week internship in area businesses. During the time of the grant, over fifteen major corporations sponsored women interns.

Improving Higher Education–Business Project Procedures

Education projects that feature community service or practicums as part of professional development frequently rely on personal contact and informal commitments between faculty members and employers. However, other methods such as formal contracts also prove effective in designing work experiences. At Birmingham Southern College (Alabama) a contract is used to initiate agreements among students, faculty, and employers. The contract forces all parties to identify the learning outcomes expected from off-campus learning in advance of job placement. It is intended to protect students from the casualness that too often characterizes off-campus programs. Clear ideas are established about the work experience in advance of the student's first day on the job. Using this approach, in 1979 Birmingham Southern sponsored 238 student projects ranging from internships in a public radio station to the study of primate behavior in a nearby zoo.

At Bay de Noc Community College (Escanaba, Michigan) the contract is a central feature in a one-year program that helps students become employable. Students complement classroom learning with twenty to thirty hours a week of work with employers to learn particular trades. In the fall of 1980, sixty students served in "externships" in fifty-six different businesses in rural Michigan. Following the one-year program, 88 percent of the students found jobs. Students in the program indicate that without the job component they would never have considered college. Employers indicate that they would not have hired the students off the street, but the combined training and education produces an "effective employee" from their point of view. All employers who have sponsored students since the program's inception in 1976 have continued to sponsor students. One modification that followed the two-year grant has been the addition of a career development course to prepare students for the work setting prior to the apprenticeship, an approach that many programs come to recognize as valuable after their first few years of operation.

Many small schools are simply unable to initiate and sustain the staff and costs associated with developing off-campus programs. Colleges in rural locations face particular difficulties in developing a wide range of work experiences for their students. Two projects supported by the fund from 1974 to 1976 addressed these problems by creating statewide and metropolitan-wide off-campus programs for students. A central office at Virginia State College administers a program on behalf of a voluntary consortium of public and private institutions throughout the state. The central office is able to assess manpower needs, maintain contact with employers, and provide technical assistance to faculty at participating institutions. Employers express satisfaction with the continuity and simplicity of working with one administrator rather than many faculty from different institutions. Students from institutions with different resources all have a chance to secure work experiences not normally available. A similar approach has also been attempted in an urban environment. The Chicago Urban Corps works with area institutions to develop an intercollegiate mechanism to administer internships. The Urban Corps found colleges receptive to the idea but encountered and overcame practical administrative questions such as "How can credit be given on the college transcript if the internship is not in the college catalog?"

At Polytechnic Institute (New York City) minority women with a two-year technical degree from community colleges are recruited and earn a B.A. and M.A. in three years. The specially developed program features an internship, and the director reports that many businesses attempt to hire the women before they complete the technical degree program. Successful degree programs like this demonstrate the importance of carefully defining real and important needs of specific audiences before committing institutional resources in more general ways.

Next Steps

Innovations in higher education–employer programs directly affecting learners need to proceed in two main directions. First, the successful experimentation and demonstration projects being conducted throughout the nation must be disseminated and must become more of the accepted curriculum in which students learn and faculty teach in higher education institutions. The fund is supporting projects for this purpose through three "network" organizations expert in improving the quality and utility of experiential education programs: the Council for the Advancement of Experiential Learning (CAEL), the National Society for Internships and Experiential Education (NSIEE), and the Western Interstate Commission on Higher Education (WICHE). Reform and innovation has been received reluctantly by most, enthusiastically by a few. Those proportions must be reversed.

Secondly, the workplace itself is the next frontier for advocates of lifelong learning opportunities. Employers and higher educators together must come to grips with the concept of "competent workers and managers." Employer, union, and employee assumptions about appropriate standards of competence are driving forces in the debates over education and training strategies. Is competence the ability to accomplish a current job up to agreed-upon standards? Is competence the ability to take on a variety of tasks, to work with others as a team, to grow in a job even at the risk of growing out of the firm? Different consequences for employer-employee and for business–higher education relations are buried in the answers to such questions. Answers will provide both sectors with a framework for more effective use of each other's resources, including more such clearly underused programs as cooperative education and tuition aid.

References

Fund for the Improvement in Postsecondary Education. *Resources for Change: A Guide to Projects, 1979–1980*. Washington, D.C.: U.S. Government Printing Office, 1980.

Fund for the Improvement in Postsecondary Education. *Resources for Change: A Guide to Projects, 1980–1981*. Washington, D.C.: U.S. Government Printing Office, 1981.

Lynn A. DeMeester has served for eleven years in the federal government in addition to conducting training in the private sector and teaching in the public schools. Since 1974, she has worked as an education program specialist with the Fund for the Improvement of Postsecondary Education, monitoring many projects featuring collaborations between colleges and employers. She holds an M.A. in Human Resources Development from George Washington University and is currently a doctoral student in public administration at George Mason University.

*Employee desire for academic credit can be a key
element in creating productive programs and
communication between business and higher
education. Monitoring the quality of corporate
training is essential.*

College Credit for
Corporate Training

John J. McGarraghy
Kevin P. Reilly

Educational activities conducted by business and industry are part of
perhaps the largest segment of postsecondary education in the nation—
that which is made up of a variety of noncollegiate organizations. These
organizations, whose primary focus is not education, include government
agencies, labor unions, professional and trade associations, and cultural
institutions.

United States business and industry offer different forms of educational opportunities to their employees and for a variety of purposes. Many
programs provide job-related training to teach new employees specific
skills or to keep older employees up to date on new products, production
methods, and government regulations. Often these courses deal with
college-level subject matter and are taught in a conventional manner, with
textbooks, lectures and class discussions, reading assignments, papers or
projects to be submitted, and evaluation of student performance. Frequently the courses incorporate innovative instructional approaches specifically geared to the subject matter being covered. Companies also use
other types of instructional approaches including computer-assisted
instruction, structured on-the-job training, and correspondence courses.

G. Gold (Ed.), *New Directions for Experiential Learning: Business and Higher Education—
Towards New Alliances*, no. 13. San Francisco: Jossey-Bass, September 1981.

Despite the college-level content, format, and high quality of many of the educational programs conducted by business and industry, until recently there had been no systematic, organized way to relate them to the country's traditional higher education system. As a result, company employees were not achieving due academic recognition for the knowledge and competencies gained through these programs. Also, there has been unnecessary duplication of educational costs and services.

In 1974 the New York State Board of Regents began the nationwide Program on Noncollegiate Sponsored Instruction to respond to this situation. The purpose of the program is to review formal educational programs and courses sponsored by business and industry and other noncollegiate organizations and to make appropriate credit recommendations for the courses evaluated. The credit recommendations are intended to guide colleges and universities as they consider awarding credit to persons who have successfully completed the courses.

The program is based on the position that it is sound educational practice to grant academic credit for quality educational programs conducted by companies and other noncollegiate organizations, provided that the courses are at the college level and that the credit is appropriate to an individual's educational degree plan.

The approach of recommending credit for courses sponsored by business and industry and other noncollegiate organizations began with the American Council on Education (ACE). Since the end of World War II, ACE has evaluated military educational programs to assist colleges and universities by providing recommendations for granting credit for such experiences and has periodically published these recommendations in a national guide. The program tested this evaluation system in the civilian sector in a pilot study initiated in 1974. In late 1974, ACE joined the state of New York in the conduct of the program. The joint operation of the program continued until September 1977, when ACE withdrew and began to operate its own independent national program (see American Council on Education, 1980).

Since the New York-based program began, 1,680 courses have been evaluated for 139 noncollegiate organizations and 1,476 courses have been recommended for credit. An estimated 100,000 persons participate in the courses annually. The course descriptions and credit recommendations have been published in five editions of *A Guide to Educational Programs in Noncollegiate Organizations* (The University of the State of New York . . . , 1980a), which is distributed to colleges and universities throughout the country.

The program evaluates courses for companies throughout the nation, including American Telephone and Telegraph, Corning Glass, Eastman Kodak, Equitable Life Insurance, Grumman Aerospace, Manufacturers Hanover Trust, McGraw-Hill, Merrill Lynch, Mobil, Pepsi-Cola,

Sperry Corporation, Union Carbide, and Western Electric. Many of the courses are in subjects related to business: accounting, banking, computer science, electrical engineering, finance, industrial technology, life insurance, management, and secretarial science.

The New York State Board of Regents took the leadership in developing this national program for a variety of reasons. The Regents have a long-standing commitment to a higher education system that provides increased access and more options to students of all ages, not least of which are the large group of working adults who want to pursue formal academic credentials. Moreover, there is a vast array of educational activities going on in New York State conducted by companies reaching a nationwide, and even an international, audience. Also, when the program began in 1974, many colleges and universities were seeking ways to assess the prior learning that students were acquiring in the workplace, so the academic climate in the state was favorable to the evaluation of noncollegiate instruction. The following three examples illustrate the type of work the program has accomplished with corporations that serve a nationwide audience.

Work with Organizations Nationally

Xerox Corporation is a multinational organization operating in over 113 countries in the areas of copiers/duplicators, information processing, reprographics, education, publishing, aerospace, and medical diagnostics. Xerox offers a variety of residential training programs to employees from the United States, Canada, and other countries, mainly at the company's International Center for Training and Management Development in Leesburg, Virginia and at facilities in Rochester, New York. Each group or division within the corporation conducts training programs for its employees.

Since 1975, the program has evaluated and recommended for credit a range of computer science, electrical technology management, and psychology courses offered by the Personnel Education and Development Center of Xerox's General Services Division (GSD) and by the National Service/Distribution-Continuing Education Program and the Personnel Management Training of the company's Information Systems Group (ISG). GSD provides telecommunications, payroll, management consulting, data processing, and other services to other groups within the corporation. ISG, which markets and services all Xerox copier and duplicator products within the United States, is the corporation's largest division, with 15,000 employees nationwide.

As a result of the program's credit recommendations for its courses, Xerox has developed a cooperative relationship with the Regents External Degree Program (REX), a fully accredited national college program, which is also New York-based. Xerox approached REX because the company had a problem commonly shared by many other employers—their employees, particularly those with longevity and experience but few credentials, felt that the lack of a college degree was hurting their chance for career mobility.

REX allows adults to earn degrees through a variety of methods, including courses (classroom or correspondence) taken from any regionally accredited college, or from nationwide proficiency exams, military education, special assessment, and employer courses with credit recommendations from the Program on Noncollegiate Sponsored Instruction. In short, an employee can take an assortment of academic experiences and fit them into the framework of a regents external associate or bachelor's degree. Since REX offers no courses of its own, all credits brought to REX are "transfer credits." With no limit on the number of transfer credits REX will accept, people with a lot of credits may find themselves very close to a REX degree. In some cases, the previous credits may even satisfy all degree requirements. In any event, Xerox employees have an obvious headstart on earning a college degree because of the credits they can gain for the corporation's courses, which have been evaluated by the program.

A formal link between the Regents and the Xerox Corporation was established in August 1980, in which Xerox staff in 140 branches across the country have been trained to serve as local contacts for information on REX.

The General Electric Company (GE) is another corporation with which the program has had a long working relationship. GE is primarily engaged in developing, manufacturing, and marketing a wide variety of products used in the generation, transmission, distribution, control, and utilization of electricity. As a result of corporate research and development, GE has also developed other businesses in such areas as communications, plastics, medical systems, aircraft engines, and ship propulsion systems. Domestic employment is approximately 300,000 persons in forty-seven GE divisions throughout the country.

GE offers many courses to its employees to help accelerate their professional and managerial career development. Whether the courses are single offerings or are part of an integrated program of study, they are all designed to help individual employees perform more effectively on current jobs, prepare for new jobs, or gain greater personal satisfaction from their work. All of the GE courses or programs that have been evaluated by the program are coordinated from GE locations in New York State but serve company employees nationwide.

One GE program that has been evaluated and received graduate credit recommendations is the advanced course in engineering. It was originally established in 1923 to supply General Electric with engineers having sufficient depth and breadth of technical understanding to make basic contributions in the development of new or improved products. The advanced course is a three and one-half-year program consisting of the company-taught courses and periods of formal academic study on campus. The course material is continuously reviewed, revised, and updated. It includes pertinent basics, state-of-the-art analytical techniques, and topical emphasis relative to changing business needs and products. The advanced course is conducted at eleven GE locations throughout the United States in cooperation with some fifteen universities. GE's corporate-level technical education program manager directly negotiated these relationships with each of the universities, using the program's credit recommendation decision as a "credibility" factor.

A final example of out-of-state work by the program is with the Electric Boat Division of the General Dynamics Corporation. General Dynamics, with corporate headquarters in St. Louis, Missouri, is a major developer and builder of weapons systems. The various divisions of the corporation also produce commercial aircraft, commercial ships, communication equipment, and mineral services.

The Electric Boat Division, located in Groton, Connecticut, is a pioneer designer and builder of submarines. The company has placed particular emphasis on continued education as one means for understanding the rapid technological changes and state of the art in shipbuilding. The extensive offering of semester-length training programs is just one demonstration of the importance placed on continued education of the employees. The division also provides preemployment training, on-the-job training, an apprentice school, tuition reimbursement for out-of-plant education, and special high school education opportunities.

The program originally discussed its evaluation and credit recommendation system with the division in summer 1980 at the request of the Connecticut Board of State Academic Awards, since Connecticut does not administer a similar program but has many companies that conduct courses for their employees. (The program had already evaluated courses for the Southern New England Telephone Company, which is headquartered in New Haven, Connecticut.) Once Electric Boat decided to have the program evaluate a group of its courses, the Connecticut Board assisted in identifying evaluators from colleges and universities in Connecticut. Also, the Connecticut Board will accept for credit towards its external degrees the Electric Boat computer science courses, which the program has now evaluated and recommended for credit. In the near future, Electric Boat plans to submit to the program additional courses in management and technical subjects for evaluation.

Uses of Credit Recommendations

Follow-up Studies. In the fall of 1976, the program began a one-year study, under a contract with the National Institute of Education, to investigate whether the credit recommendations were being used and how they have affected colleges and universities, companies, other types of noncollegiate organizations, and individual users of the credit recommendations.

A majority (68 percent) of the 170 higher education institutions in New York State that responded to the survey reported that they had an institution-wide or department policy on using the credit recommendations or were developing such a policy. That represented nearly a doubling of the number of colleges granting credit for noncollegiate-sponsored courses since the program began in 1974. (A more recent informal survey reported that more than 350 colleges and universities in the country have made use of the program's recommendations.)

Out of the forty-one companies and other types of noncollegiate organizations surveyed, more than half reported that enrollment in the courses that had received recommendations had increased and student performance had improved. Thirty-six percent of the responding organizations were revising additional courses in accordance with the program's evaluative criteria. Seventy-two percent of the organizations now use these same evaluative criteria when they develop new courses for their employees.

The 469 responding students reported that they received credit for 82 percent of the courses that they submitted to colleges during the 1975–76 academic year. Courses were submitted to colleges both in New York State and in other states throughout the country. Thirty-five percent of the responding students who were not enrolled in college at the time the credit recommendations were established reported that they were motivated to enroll in a college course or degree program because they received credit for a company course they had previously completed. Because most of the respondents were already enrolled in college, the credit granted to most students for the recommended courses was used to accelerate their study in college programs.

The program initiated a second study of participants during the 1977–78 academic year. It was a substantially modified version of the first study, but it was able to focus on employees in thirteen organizations representing a cross-section of those served by the program. The findings of the second study thoroughly support those of the first study and show that the credit recommendations had benefited students in other ways. Forty-eight percent of them used the credit recommendations to gain job advancements, 8 percent used them for salary increments, and 7 percent for professional licensure or certification.

Other Program Services. The two studies showed that, generally, the program was meeting the objectives for which it was established. At the same time, they revealed a need for program staff to provide additional information and assistance to companies and employees to ensure more effective and widespread use of the credit recommendations. As a result, the program published a manual for company staff titled *Using the Credit Recommendations: A Handbook for Noncollegiate Organizations* (The University of the State of New York . . . , 1980b). The handbook explains ways to publicize the credit recommendations internally and externally, describes the information that should be provided on a student transcript, and suggests steps that a company can take in developing a working relationship with a college and the different kinds of services a college might provide as part of this relationship.

Program staff regularly respond to requests from colleges for information on the evaluation and credit recommendation system and on specific courses that have been evaluated. They also refer companies and employees to specific college staff members who will be of assistance in gaining credit for program-recommended courses. If individual employees have difficulty in getting credit recommendations accepted by colleges, the program helps their companies develop cooperative relationships with colleges or educational advisement services for their employees. Finally, the program holds regional conferences periodically to bring together staff from local colleges and representatives of companies that have had courses evaluated. The conferences explore ways to meet the educational needs of company employees.

Educational Advisement in the Employment Setting

Besides demonstrating that working adults needed more information and counseling on the credit recommendation system, the follow-up studies indicated that many full-time workers who expressed the desire to continue their education were not taking advantage of the range of educational opportunities available to them. In response, the program developed models of educational advisement in different types of employment settings. Supported by the Fund for the Improvement of Postsecondary Education, the project has established educational advisement services in the Albany Department of Human Resources (the Albany City CETA Program), the New York State Department of Labor, and the New York Telephone Company. Selected employees in each organization have been trained as educational advisers, gaining the skills and knowledge necessary to manage an advisement center, to assist other employees in their educational planning, and to develop cooperative working relationships between the organization and local educational institutions. The project has also worked with these advisers to establish inventories of educational resources for the regions in which the organizations are located.

The project has shown that the workplace is a familiar and relatively comfortable place for working people to discuss and plan education and career goals. Moreover, it is usually easier for them to explore such goals with persons whom they regard as peers than with academic counselors who may seem threatening. And they can see and be motivated by the educational accomplishments of their peers, an especially important factor for women and older persons. Data collected in the follow-up studies support this view. A majority of people interviewed during the studies were motivated to return to school because someone at work had told them about available college programs and about the advantage of receiving credit for company courses based on the credit recommendations. Many of these people had been away from school for more than fifteen years and seemed to trust the advice of the training or personnel staff in their organizations. Repeated throughout the personal interviews of students was the message that they had first learned that they could handle college-level work by taking courses conducted by their organization that had received college credit recommendations. Because this experience took place at work, the educational counseling there had credibility for them.

The advisement centers established in the three organizations served some 1,750 clients in the fifteen months they were monitored closely by project staff. The second follow-up study made clear that the credit recommendations were being used by a younger group, in lower-paying jobs, with less educational experience than those surveyed in the previous study. This newer student group, which should be a growing segment of the college-going population in the 1980s, is thus composed of persons who, in all likelihood, will need the help a worksite educational broker can offer. In the New York Telephone Company, for instance, the majority of employees served by the educational advisers have been nonmanagement women. Demand for in-person consultations with the Telephone Company's eight advisers has increased to the point that at this time appointments must be made two and a half months in advance of the consultation.

Since each of the organizations is different in mission, structure, and population, each has developed its own style in delivering brokering services. The Albany CETA educational adviser has worked out of two locations in the city. The Labor Department advisers have central offices in cities across upstate New York—Albany, Binghamton, Buffalo, Rochester, Syracuse, and Utica. The adviser headquartered in each city travels to branch offices in a large district surrounding his central office. The Telephone Company advisers see most of their clients in one of the corporation's main New York City offices, but they serve the entire metropolitan area. Eight of the company's human resource development specialists are part-time educational advisers. Likewise in the Labor Department, seven training technicians have taken on the role of educational adviser in addition to their other responsibilities. The Albany CETA educational adviser works full-time at the job. This diversity helps ensure that these model educational brokering centers will be replicable or adaptable for use by a wide variety of other noncollegiate organizations. The Deputy Commissioner of the Albany Department of Human Resources has stated that because of the project, educational advisement is "now an integral part of our agency services" for CETA enrollees.

Problem Issues

Several important issues have been addressed regularly by evaluation teams from 1974 to the present, although these issues by no means arise in dealing with all, or even most, noncollegiate organizations.

Some company courses contain more contact hours than the traditional forty-hour (more or less) semester course featured in many colleges, but may receive a recommendation for the same number of credits (usually three) as the forty-hour course. Evaluators have given two main reasons for this apparent imbalance. One is that a segment of the contact time in some company courses is given over to content that is "company specific"— particular to a company's policies or machines, perhaps—or at least is not content of the type covered in a college course in the same field. The other reason is that the "extra" contact hours in some company courses may compensate for fewer hours devoted to out-of-class assignments. An instructor in a noncollegiate sponsored course may not be able to demand the level of output in homework assignments from his working adult students that a college professor would from a full-time student. In fact, labor union contracts sometimes prohibit mandatory assignments that cannot be completed during working hours.

The issue of instructors' credentials had to be addressed squarely at the outset of the program. Would academic evaluators be willing to recommend credit for courses taught by instructors who in some instances did not have the number or the kind of degrees that a four-year college instructor might be expected to have? Would an evaluation team's decision to recommend credit or to withhold recommendation turn on whether an instructor had earned a master's degree or a Ph.D. in a certain subject? Evaluators need assurance that instructors have acquired adequate expertise in their teaching specialties, and that assurance can be provided in a variety of ways. An academic credential is one way; others include inspection of all the tools and methods used by the instructor in delivering a course, notably the written response to graded student exams and projects, scrutiny of instructor selection procedures, and interviews with course administrators and with instructors themselves. Evaluators found that they could rely on these techniques in judging whether an instructor's expertise was of the caliber required to teach a college-level course. They also found that a sizable percentage of companies engaged in employee education offer instructors formal training in communicating their expertise, that is, in the art of teaching.

Two other potential problems inherent in the attempt to translate noncollegiate sponsored instruction into academic credit involve teaching methods and student performance evaluation tools. Some noncollegiate organizations tend to employ a number of different types of instruction in one course, from lectures (delivered by an instructor or presented on videotape) to supervised laboratory work and workshops, to seminar-style discussions. Companies sometimes build an on-the-job training component into their course curricula. Academic evaluators committed to a lecture format have had to adjust to this more eclectic approach.

Lack of an appropriate mechanism to gauge student performance will prevent a credit recommendation from being made. There have been instances of company courses that appear to be eminently eligible for a credit recommendation in every way except that they do not include some test of student learning. Inappropriateness of the testing tool has often been one of the major factors in decisions not to recommend courses for credit; absence of testing tool has been a chief reason that more courses have not been submitted for evaluation. Training directors sometimes want to avoid introducing a student performance test into a course because they fear that it will encourage an unhealthy competition among employees, who may be from different levels and divisions in the corporate structure, or that it will discourage the enrollment of employees they would like to see take the course. These can be legitimate concerns.

One way to come to grips with this problem (certainly not to solve it completely) is to install an optional student performance evaluation. Those employees who want to use the credit recommendation in a degree program can take the exam or write up the case study, while those who do not intend to use the recommendation need not. When the testing mechanism has been found to be inappropriate, without sufficient depth or breadth of coverage, for example, evaluators have on occasion established a conditional credit recommendation. In these cases, the company must resubmit the testing mechanism revised along the lines suggested by the evaluators. Upon approval of the revision, the conditional credit recommendation becomes operative.

Another obstacle to the establishment of a credit recommendation for a company training program was alluded to earlier. An in-house course that is thoroughly geared to meeting a particular set of internal corporate needs will most likely not prove transferable into the more generalized and theoretical college curriculum. For example, a course entitled something like "Labor Relations" was once presented to the program for evaluation. During the site review, the evaluation team discovered that the course focused almost entirely on the personnel policies and procedures of the corporation offering it, so the team felt it could not recommend the course for college credit. It should be said that the evaluators' decision does not imply that the course did not serve the company's purposes well. In this and similar cases, evaluators are indicating only that such courses do not resemble college courses taught in the comparable subject areas.

The Future

The demand for the kind of linkages the program has developed between noncollegiate organizations and colleges seems to be growing around the country as well as in New York. In the case of Electric Boat, the program was asked to bring its evaluation expertise to a company that does not operate at all within New York State. The program hosted a conference in 1979, supported by the National Institute of Education, to discuss the implications of its follow-up studies with officials from higher education agencies in other states. Seven states sent representatives to learn about the program's credit recommendation system. During 1980, the program performed evaluations for the Vermont Criminal Justice Training Council, the agency that conducts training for the Vermont State Police. Representatives of the Washington State Public Power Supply System recently visited program offices to discuss their interest in the evaluation of their nuclear reactor operator training program.

A relatively recent program innovation within New York State is the evaluation of training offered by CETA prime sponsors in terms of postsecondary, and in some instances secondary, credit. To date, more than fifty CETA training programs have been recommended for credit as the result of a contract between the program and the New York State Department of Labor.

Some writers on career development argue persuasively that the average worker in the coming decades will hold up to eight different jobs in a lifetime. These jobs will not necessarily be much alike because the increasingly rapid pace of technological change will require constant creation of new job functions. If these prognosticators are close to being correct, much training and retraining for those new functions will be needed. Given such a scenario, the system the program has developed for linking colleges and universities with education provided at the workplace could become a significant part of the vital national effort to keep job skills current.

References

American Council on Education. *The National Guide to Credit Recommendations for Noncollegiate Courses.* Washington, D.C.: American Council on Education 1980.

The University of the State of New York, Program on Noncollegiate Sponsored Instruction. *A Guide to Educational Programs in Noncollegiate Organizations.* (5th ed.) Albany: The University of the State of New York, 1980a.

The University of the State of New York, Program on Noncollegiate Sponsored Instruction. *Using the Credit Recommendations: A Handbook for Noncollegiate Organizations.* Albany: The University of the State of New York, 1980b.

*John J. McGarraghy is director of the Division of Academic
Program Review in the New York State Education
Department, which oversees chartering of postsecondary
institutions in the state and registering of their degree
programs. He was the first director of the New York Regents
Program on Noncollegiate Sponsored Instruction, serving in
that capacity from 1974 to 1979.*

*Kevin P. Reilly is director of the New York Regents Program
on Noncollegiate Sponsored Instruction. Before joining the
Regents' staff, he taught literature, composition, and
technical writing at the University of Minnesota, where he
served as assistant to the director of Undergraduate Study in
English.*

Every community differs in its mix of business,
labor, education, and governmental resources.
Only within local labor markets can these resources
be linked to anticipate future needs as well as to deal
with current problems.

Partners in
Economic Development

Regina M. J. Kyle

We have entered a period when business, government, and labor have
acknowledged their mutual need to work together to revitalize the American economy (Dunlop, 1980). For example, a "blue-ribbon" joint labor-
management committee was recently formed at the national level to work
out problems of mutual concern. The special issue of *Business Week* (June
18, 1980) devoted to economic reindustrialization stressed the importance
of a new "social contract" among groups with power to affect economic
activity.

One of the key elements necessary for economic revitalization is the
development of mechanisms to manage the local labor market. This can be
done only through approaches that recognize and build on the systematic
nature of the local economy and the resources already present within it. In
this process, colleges and universities have an active role to play. This
chapter proposes the concept of Human Resources Management Centers as
a pragmatic mechanism through which business, government, and higher
education can cooperate to effectively use our most important capital
resource, human talent, and energy. This is the true "wealth of nations," as
Harbison has stressed in his work (Harbison, 1973).

G. Gold (Ed.), *New Directions for Experiential Learning: Business and Higher Education—*
Towards New Alliances, no. 13. San Francisco: Jossey-Bass, September 1981.

The Economic Context

We tend to ignore the economic functions of our educational institutions. Colleges and universities are both producers and consumers of manpower, goods, and services. These functions involve them in many aspects of our economic life, but no aspect is more central to the dynamics of economic behavior than their role in the labor market.

Building on earlier analyses of institutional mission (Gollattscheck and others, 1976; Kyle, 1978, 1979), the simple model in Figure 1 illustrates how these functions relate to the various missions of individual institutions.

Figure 1. Higher Education: Sphere of Economic Functions

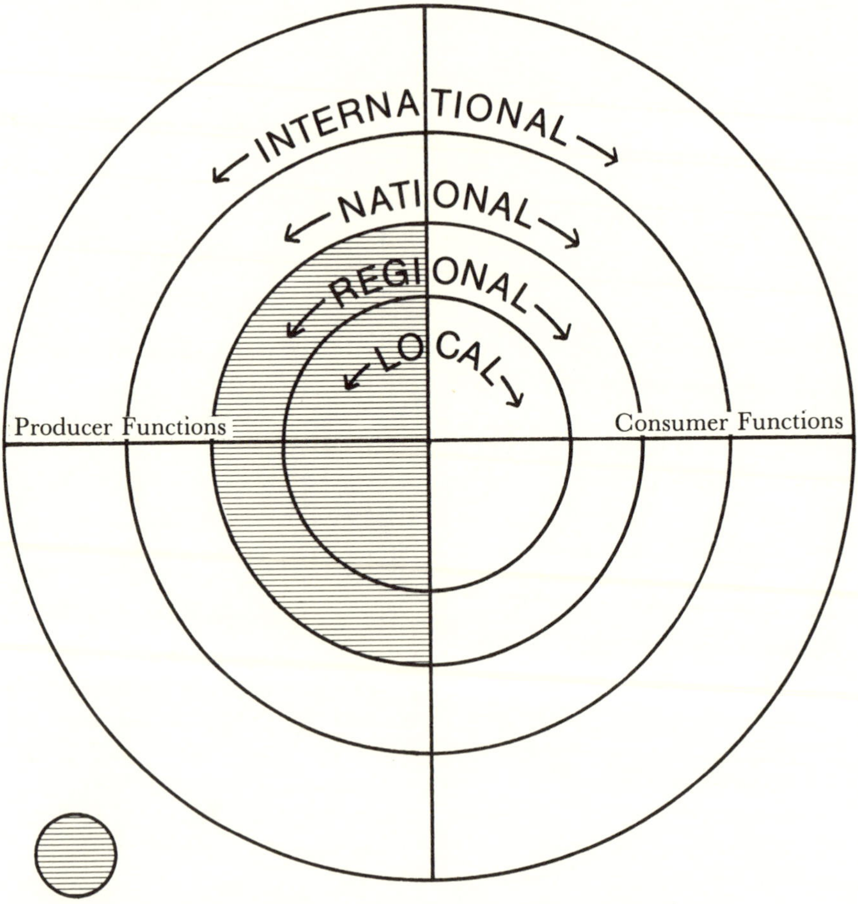

Regional and local production functions of higher education

The left side of the model represents the productive functions of the college; the right side of the resources it consumes to do this. These functions are related to four constituencies, or communities, that the college may serve in carrying out its mission: the local, regional, national, and international. This chapter is concerned primarily with the left-hand side, the producer side, at the local and regional levels. Two examples, drawn from actual situations, show how the model can be used to profile a college's present activities in terms of the communities they serve.

Two colleges, *A* and *B*, are located in the same city. Their economic production profiles are shown in Figure 2. College *A* is a major research university with a commitment to serving national and international con-

Figure 2. Economic Production Profiles of Colleges A and B

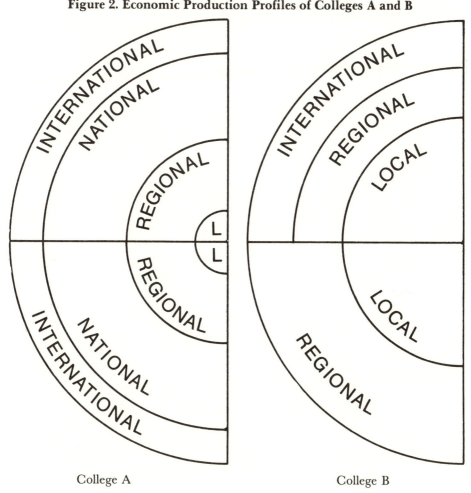

College A   College B

stituencies. It draws its student body from a national constituency, with large numbers of international students and only moderate regional and local representation. Its research produces goods and services in areas of concern to national and international groups in development and health care. It is also involved in services to the local and regional communities, although to a lesser extent. College *B* is a community college that, like some community colleges in large urban areas, has what one might consider an atypical student profile because of its large numbers of foreign students. Its service pattern, however, is more typical of the community college, with its base in the local and regional communities.

These sample profiles are meant to reflect present conditions. If we were to look at the same two institutions at the end of World War II, we would find interesting differences. For college *A,* both the international and regional components would be less significant. For college *B,* the international component would probably be nonexistent; indeed, college *B* itself might not exist. Their current profiles reflect broad changes in the economy and in society, changes directly responsible for our present inability to manage the labor market effectively.

In thirty-five years, the worlds of education and work have been transformed almost beyond recognition. We have moved from a goods-producing to a service economy. Between 1947 and 1977, the civilian labor force grew by forty million, with large numbers of women entering and remaining in it. Technological development, the rebuilding of the industrial base in Europe and Japan after World War II, economic and social change in Third World nations, and the building of supranational economic networks converged to bring about a revolution in both products and processes through the global integration of the economy (Drucker, 1980; Kyle, forthcoming; OECD, 1980).

Almost without noticing it, American industry shifted its manpower requirements, using more people with higher levels of education than ever before. In 1952 the median number of school years completed by those in the labor force was 10.9; in 1977 it was 12.6. Among professional, technical, and managerial workers, the shift between 1948 and 1977 was from 12.8 to 16.0 years and among craftworkers, operatives, and laborers from 9.0 to 12.2 (Bureau of Labor Statistics, 1978).

The changing needs of industry, combined with federal policies related to economic and defense issues, triggered the expansion of higher education. Beginning with the GI Bill in 1944 and continuing through defense-related legislation aimed at developing technological superiority over the Russians after Sputnik and into the economic focus of social legislation from the Manpower Development and Training Act (MDTA) through the Comprehensive Employment and Training Act (CETA), the federal government used colleges and universities as major instruments of defense, economic, and social policy. Colleges changed in size and control;

their student body mushroomed from 1.5 million students in 1940 to 11.4 million in 1977. The characteristics of the student body changed, with increasing numbers of part-time students, women, minorities, and older students joining the traditional eighteen to twenty-four-year-old white males of former years.

Colleges responded to new needs with new programs and new delivery systems. But just as in industry and the government, these responses have often been piecemeal and uncoordinated. Often, institutions realized only after a series of such changes over the years that they had, in fact, changed their very missions. The impact of these structural changes is usually examined and policy made at the macro level of the economy. Far too little has been done at the level of the local labor market, where strategies for change must be implemented (Barton, 1979).

Local Labor Markets

A local labor market includes all jobs and the labor force in "an economically integrated geographic unit that consists of a central city or cities, and the surrounding territory within normal commuting distance" (State of California, 1977, p. 25). This unit is really a complex system of "labor markets," including both the general area-wide or "external" labor market and the "internal" labor markets of jobs and workers within individual firms (Kerr, 1954; Doeringer and Piore, 1971). The equilibrium of the local labor market—its ability to maintain a positive, dynamic relationship between supply and demand for manpower—is dependent, among other factors, on local educational systems, both private and public, at all levels. Without a dependable source of training in basic skills, general education, and specific vocational and professional knowledge, severe dislocations are inevitable in the labor market. Present educational institutions supply this needed training with varying degrees of success and failure. While there are many individual arrangements between individual firms and particular colleges, very little has been done at the local level to establish collaborative ventures leading to the management of the general labor market.

Gross unemployment figures, whether national or local, are problematic primarily because they mask rather than reveal the true nature of supply-demand imbalances. For example, in planning a recent retraining effort in a midwestern state, the data organized at the state level were found inappropriate for planning at the local level. The data indicated needs that did not apply in particular circumstances and that in some instances no longer reflected even statewide conditions. In contrast, local economies are distinctive in their job-skill composition and the causes of unemployment. The combination of high unemployment with skills shortages may have many causes in a given community:

- Insufficient jobs
- The structure of work and compensation
- The physical location of jobs and people in relation to transportation
- Inadequate or inappropriate skills and skill levels among potential workers
- Inadequate labor market information systems
- Inadequate labor market management systems.

The last three items are problems whose solutions lie partly in the hands of colleges and universities. In conjunction with the business community, labor, and government, they have the resources to change present situations. Our present economic problems have become serious enough to force leaders in business, education, government, and labor to recognize the need for policies and strategies at the local level.

Managing the Local Labor Market

The Human Resources Management Center (HRMC) is a strategic model for the management of economic dislocations resulting from both structural and cyclical imbalances in the local labor market. While its first concern is the external labor market in a specific geographic area, the HRMC has the capability of serving the internal markets of individual firms as well. Mobility within the firm is governed by a series of policies and "traditions" relating to human resource development that give the firm its particular character. The relationship between the internal market of the individual firm and the external local labor market is a complex one since the internal market is part of the external market. They are interdependent and interactive.

Structure and Functions of the HRMC. The primary role of the HRMC will be to provide the information base and technical assistance needed to avoid serious disruptions in the local economy and to promote a condition of dynamic equilibrium in the supply-demand patterns of manpower in a particular area. Each HRMC will have three interactive units to perform an integrated set of functions necessary to accomplish these ends, as shown in Figure 3.

Unit One is the data collection and analysis group. It will build the model of the local economy, collect and analyze relevant data, develop documents to assist the planning and decision making in Unit Two, and provide long-term (futures) thinking about evolving patterns in the local labor market. Nothing closely approximating this type of operation currently exists at the local level. Unit One is the cornerstone of the HRMC; without it the center will be unable to achieve its goals.

Many of the pieces needed to construct Unit One already exist in some fashion in present federal, state, and local agencies and in institutions

Figure 3. HRMC: Preliminary Model

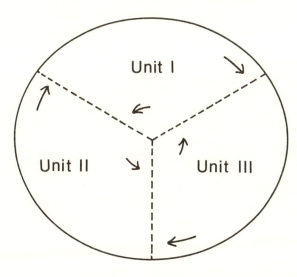

of higher education. Present infrastructures will need to be modified and current resources shifted to support this. In addition to the regular process of data collection and analysis, it is particularly important that one person in this unit be responsible for tracking developments in technology and developing scenarios showing the possible impacts of these developments on the local economic scene. These scenarios will serve as an "early-warning" system in a period of rapid change and sudden dislocations.

Unit Two, the leadership council, will bring together community leaders who can deliver the support of important groups within the area: business, labor, education, and government. The leadership council is key to both the establishment and effective functioning of the HRMC. This is the basic decision-making unit in the center.

Based on the data and analyses provided by Unit One, the leadership council will select those dislocations needing cooperative intervention. Strategies will be developed for correcting the problem and an appropriate mix of remedies selected. Unit Two will also be concerned with long-range and strategic planning.

Unit Three, the technical assistance unit, will provide services at cost to individual business enterprises, schools and colleges, government agencies, labor unions, and other local organizations. These services might include helping a firm with impact analysis, a college with community needs analysis, or any group with a full human resource management plan. Unit Three will broker the development of special courses needed to avoid labor shortages. For example, where computer specialists and software developers are in short supply, they would assist the appropriate colleges to shape programs to retrain teachers and others for new careers in this area. With retraining becoming a key strategy in any comprehensive human resource policy, this function should take on increasing importance. This unit would require subsidy in the start-up stage, but should become self-supporting by the third year of operation.

This description outlines the major functions of the HRMC. A full description appears in a recently completed report for Harvard University (Kyle, forthcoming).

Colleges and the HRMC. This brief outline of the structure and functions of the HRMC suggests a number of important contributions that colleges might make to the effective functioning of the center. Depending on the resources of the individual institution, a college might be an active participant at the planning, development, and operating stages of the project.

In an earlier suggestion for the planning of a pilot project for a comprehensive labor market information system at the local level, Yavitz has suggested using a university research team in developing the basic inventory of current available information (Yavitz and others, 1973). The Yavitz proposal, while less comprehensive than the HRMC, addresses many of the major issues related to the need for an effective data base and suggests a "consortium" approach not unlike the proposed collaborative one. Colleges and universities should be represented on the policy planning group in the early stages of development and their expertise should be tapped for the research teams building the data bases for the center.

At the operational level, the knowledge and skills of the higher education sector will be needed in all three units. Centers will differ from one geographic region to another because of the existence or lack of certain resources; patterns of college and university participation may not follow a single model. A single academic institution, a group of institutions, or a combined government agency–university unit might be responsible for the operation of Unit One. Individual institutions will be represented on the leadership council in Unit Two and appropriate faculty and programs will be utilized for the technical assistance services provided by Unit Three. Participation in the HRMC will open up new opportunities for colleges and universities, as well as enable them to carry out more effectively some of their basic functions as partners in the economic system.

The HRMC is a comprehensive proposal requiring initial stimulus at the national level and catalytic action by leaders of the private and public sectors. Because it is a multicomponent, strategic approach to the critical problems of recurrent dislocations in the labor market, it will take several years to develop effective working models. It is important, therefore, for individual colleges to continue to collaborate with government, business, and labor in attacking single aspects of the problem. In the process, they can develop the mutual trust and experience needed to take on more complex responsibilities and tasks.

Colleges and Human Resources Management

What can colleges and universities do before the HRMC becomes a reality? For some, the answer to this question means continuing to do some things they are already engaged in; for others it may mean examining their role in the local community and using their resources in new ways. In each community, there are particular labor market analysis, planning, and training needs that individual institutions can help to fill.

For example, in Massachusetts the High Technology Council has been deeply concerned about the lack of high-powered part-time professional programs for masters-level work in engineering and computer science. It has, so far, been relatively unsuccessful in persuading University X, whose profile resembles College A in our model, to respond to this need. In the same state, the Wang Institute, founded by Wang Laboratories, emerged from the need for advanced education in the computer sciences, which present institutions were unable to meet. As we move more and more toward an information-based economy, as technological breakthroughs affect production processes, as revolutions in the workplace such as that now under way in the organization and functioning of the business office occur, colleges and universities will need to play a more conscious role in working with industry to prepare men and women to respond to these changes with the necessary knowledge and skills.

Two of the most elaborate corporate–higher education programs are those of Polaroid and Kimberly-Clark, both documented in case studies by the National Institute for Work and Learning (Knox, 1979; Rosow, 1979). The Kimberly-Clark plan gives us some insight into both the company's attitude toward education as a tool of human resource management and how it used local institutions to develop a comprehensive approach.

A member of the original company team noted, "The company's top-level managers were absolutely convinced that education is either *the* or *an extremely* significant variable in the development of Kimberly-Clark employees" (Rosow, 1979, p. xii). This belief, not always so explicitly documented, lies behind all industry education programs.

The Kimberly-Clark Educational Opportunities Plan draws on local educational resources wherever the company is located. In its headquarters in Neenah, Wisconsin, this has meant developing linkages primarily with various branches of the University of Wisconsin, which has an independent track record of providing extensive services to adult learners.

New arrangements are emerging regularly in areas all over the country. Hallmark Inc. has a cooperative program with the University of Missouri, Kansas City; AT&T Long Lines cooperates with George

Washington University in the District of Columbia. Recently Fairchild Industries has developed two programs: the first, with the University of Maryland at College Park to train its engineers; the second, as part of the Piedmont Area Evening Degree Association (PAEDA), formed by a number of employers in North Carolina with High Point College, a four-year private liberal arts college. This program offers employees of the participating companies the opportunity to earn an undergraduate degree at night at locations provided by the association.

Partners with Labor. Educational institutions have also joined forces with organized labor to provide opportunities for union members. The most extensively documented case is that of the Education Fund of District Council 37 (Shore, 1979). The fund, provided through the collective bargaining agreement of American Federation of State, County, and Municipal Employees' (AFSCME) District Council 37 in New York, is administered by the union and involves work with colleges such as Hofstra University and the College of New Rochelle.

Other major cooperative labor-college programs include the Labor-Liberal Arts program of Cornell's School of Industrial and Labor Relations and the Labor Studies program of Wayne State University in Detroit.

These brief examples indicate some of the directions that work-related education programs have been taking in the last ten years. They only hint at the extent of the involvement of educational institutions in the management of the internal labor market of individual establishments. In their work on internal labor markets, Doeringer and Piore noted the importance of on-the-job training in the regulation of the internal market (Doeringer and Piore, 1971). They were referring primarily to informal, on-the-job training in manufacturing establishments. Since that time, we have become much more aware of the extent to which structured and formal programs, using both in-house resources and those of educational institutions within the community, have become controlling factors in regulating mobility within the company. Almost no formal analysis has been done of this phenomenon. Case studies of individual establishments and inventories of current college and university involvement in on-site education programs and special contract arrangements with industry would shed more light in this area.

R&D Relationships. One final topic requires brief consideration here. On the producer side of the higher education economic functions model, the production of goods and services has been included as one element. Though my examples have emphasized the production of manpower, equally important is the area of knowledge generation or research and development.

The growth of R&D activities in both industry and the university has followed a pattern similar to general program growth: vertical integration within the individual organization moving slowly toward collaborative work with other organizations. The process has been much slower in R&D, for many sound reasons. However, the need to husband scarce resources and the high cost of certain types of equipment necessary for research have moved educational institutions to seek joint efforts with industry. The most noteworthy recent development in this area is happening in Minnesota.

MEIS, the Micrelectronic and Information Science Center, draws on the resources of the University of Minnesota and such companies as Control Data, Honeywell, Sperry, and 3M. The center will be jointly controlled by the university and the industries and will draw on scientists within industry as well as at the university. Laboratories in both places will be open to researchers. In addition to basic research, it is hoped that the center will increase the output of Ph.D.s in the computer sciences produced by the university. Discoveries will be licensed to small companies as well as large. The integration of R&D activities across the university and industrial sectors will present tough problems to be solved, but the potential gains for both sides and for the economy outweigh the risks.

Implications for Planning. Most of the examples of collaborative work between higher education, business, labor, and government described in this chapter have come about not as the result of conscious planning on the part of colleges and universities but as responses to individual situations and opportunities. There must always be room in an organization to do this. As Drucker (1980) has so well stated, "In turbulent times, an enterprise has to be managed *both* to withstand sudden blows and to avail itself of sudden unexpected opportunities" (p. 9). When individual responses begin to form regular patterns, it is time to incorporate them into the formal planning of the organization.

The time has come for colleges and universities to incorporate into their strategic planning carefully developed mechanisms that will allow higher education institutions to fulfill more effectively the economic functions associated with their missions. All four sets of functions have an impact on the effective management of the local labor market. To look at the activities of the college from this perspective is to give those responsible for its welfare a more complete view of the reality of what it is presently doing and the nature of possible future initiatives of both an independent and collaborative kind.

References

Barton, P. E. *The Next Step in Managing Recessions: Countercyclical Education and Training.* Washington, D.C.: The National Manpower Institute, 1979.

Bureau of Labor Statistics. *Handbook of Labor Statistics.* Bulletin 2000. Washington, D.C.: U.S. Government Printing Office, 1978.

Business Week, June 18, 1980, No. 2643.

Charner, I. *Patterns of Adult Participation in Learning Activities.* Washington, D.C.: The National Institute for Work and Learning, 1980.

Charner, I., and others. *An Untapped Resource: Negotiated Tuition-Aid in the Private Sector.* Washington, D.C.: The National Manpower Institute, 1978.

Doeringer, P., and Piore, M. *Internal Labor Markets and Manpower Analysis.* Lexington, Mass.: Heath, 1971.

Drucker, P. F. *Managing in Turbulent Times.* New York: Harper & Row, 1980.

Dunlop, J. T. (Ed.). *Business and Public Policy.* Cambridge, Mass.: Division of Research, Graduate School of Business Administration, Harvard University, 1980.

Fraser, B. S. *The Structure of Adult Learning, Education, and Training Opportunity in the United States.* Washington, D.C.: The National Institute for Work and Learning, 1980.

Ginzberg, E. (Ed.). *Employing the Unemployed.* New York: Basic Books, 1980.

Goldstein, H. *Training Provided by Industry.* Washington, D.C.: The National Institute for Work and Learning, 1980.

Gollattscheck, J. F., and others. *College Leadership for Community Renewal: Beyond Community-Based Education.* San Francisco: Jossey-Bass Publishers, 1976.

Harbison, F. H. *Human Resources as the Wealth of Nations.* New York: Oxford University Press, 1973.

Kerr, C. "The Balkanization of Labor Markets," in E. W. Bakke and others. *Labor Mobility and Economic Opportunity.* Cambridge, Mass.: Technology Press of MIT, 1954.

Knox, K. *Polaroid Corporation's Tuition Assistance Plan: A Case Study.* Washington, D.C.: The National Manpower Institute, 1979.

Kyle, R.M.J. "Planning for the 80's I." *Trendreport,* 1978, *1* (1), 3–9.

Kyle, R.M.J. "Planning for the 80's II." *TRENDS 2000,* 1979, *1* (2), 2–6.

Kyle, R.M.J. *Economic Vitality and Human Resource Management: The Education-Work Nexus.* Cambridge, Mass.: Harvard University, forthcoming.

Lusterman, S. *Education in Industry.* New York: The Conference Board, 1977.

OECD. *Technical Change and Economic Policy.* Paris, France: Organisation for Economic Co-operation and Development, 1980.

Rosow, L. A. *Kimberly-Clark Corporation's Educational Opportunities Plan: A Case Study.* Washington, D.C.: The National Manpower Institute, 1979.

Shore, J. *The Education Fund of District Council 37: A Case Study.* Washington, D.C.: National Manpower Institute, September 1979.

State of California, Central Area Labor Market Information Group. *Labor Market Review.* Sacramento: State of California, 1977/1978.

Yavitz, B., and others. *The Labor Market: An Information System.* New York: Praeger, 1973.

Regina M. J. Kyle is a management consultant in Washington, D.C. This chapter was written while she was Fellow of the National Institute for Work and Learning. She has taught on the faculties of Harvard University and the University of Texas at Dallas, where she also served as Executive Dean. She has just completed a major report on education and economic development for the Wertheim Committee at Harvard University.

*Only as investments in human resources gain a
stature equivalent to those in technology in the
economic health of organizations will innovation in
business-higher education relations move from the
periphery of corporate and university concerns
toward the center.*

Closing Thoughts

Gerard G. Gold

What will be the shape of business-higher education relationships in the
1980s? One can speculate endlessly on how those relationships might be
arranged and rearranged: corporate colleges; college admissions quotas
based on labor market projections for specific skills; federal government
financing of continuing education and training sabbaticals for workers (on
the European model); nationwide marketing of Great University Lectures
on video cassettes and discs; public financing of corporate training beyond
the partial subsidies now available; corporate-union–higher education
negotiations of internal training and promotion policies; community-
based, noncollegiate, noncredit internship networks; vastly expanded
cooperative education programs brokered through corporate-funded
community resource clearinghouses; "libraries of the future" linked to
adult learners by cable television and computer printouts.

The major problem with these speculations is that so little is known
about the scope of current interrelationships between these sectors and
other components of learning systems as they exist in communities, in
states, and nationwide. Far too little is known, for example, about the
actual breadth and depth of corporate education and training, about the
extent of higher education contracts with and services to private and public
employers, about the use of coordination units and intermediary organizations in brokering interinstitutional relationships, about the extent of
human resource development and education activities in public-sector

G. Gold (Ed.), *New Directions for Experiential Learning: Business and Higher Education—
Towards New Alliances*, no. 13. San Francisco: Jossey-Bass, September 1981.

organizations and unions, and about the probable impact of tele-communications technologies on information distribution and learning opportunities.

Studies by The Conference Board (Lusterman, 1977) and the Worker Education and Training Policies Project of the National Institute for Work and Learning (Carpenter, 1980; Charner, 1980; Fraser, 1980) are starting points, but only that. A full descriptive profile of the nationwide scene has never been available. Nor has any research attempted to place education and training needs and decisions of private-sector employers within their proper policy context. These needs and decisions, for all their interest to educators, have long been a low priority when placed in competition with issues of finance, taxes, technology, labor relations, production, and marketing. Hopefully a recently announced study sponsored by the National Institute of Education will elucidate the impact of various public policies on education and training decisions in the private sector.

Similarly in the areas of research and development and flows of human resources, we have only scratched the surface in understanding the potential value of and the potential mechanisms for greater collaboration. As Johnson and Tornatzky reported in Chapter Three, we are somewhat more informed about the policy and organizational factors influencing the funding and distribution of basic and scientific research. This knowledge is available because basic research and technological innovation have been linked since World War II to the nation's economic productivity, competitiveness in international markets, and military strength.

Only as human resources gain stature as a factor equivalent to technology in the health of individual organizations and the nation as a whole will innovation in career development methodologies move from the periphery of national corporate policy toward the center. Movement in this direction is happening if only because more sophisticated, expensive technologies require more reliable and sophisticated people to operate and manage them.

A renewed concern for quality control in manufacturing, clearly articulated in a 1980 NBC television "white paper" comparing Japanese and American management styles and techniques (National Broadcasting Company, 1980), should result in longer-term, management-sponsored research into career development patterns and organizational dynamics. Cooperative research has helped significantly to develop the discipline of organizational psychology, since the days of "scientific management" at the turn of the century and the "human relations" research of the 1930s, to the managerial style and organizational systems studies of the post–World War II period. To date, however, little of this research has been aimed directly at the interinstitutional linkages between business and higher education or between business and secondary education, where critical problems with quality control are proving costly to corporations and destructive of political support for public education.

Most perplexing, and most filled with intriguing possibilities, are the unknowns surrounding the future roles of communication technologies. Today electronic mail and instant global communications exist for large corporations while few students in secondary schools have access to computers, and many school and college faculty still rely on mimeograph machines. Entry-level jobs from secretaries to machine operators will be transformed in the next ten years. But schools and colleges cannot keep pace with either the capital investment required for new technologies or with the intellectual transformations these technologies are working on the ways people relate to each other and to information. Higher education–business relationships in all four functional areas will be affected as the nature of work and the sources of learning become more diverse. As the separation between technology-rich and technology-poor increases, will the disparities between groups of learners affiliated with those institutions also increase?

Finally, perhaps the major uncertainty of all is the future status of the financing of education, public and private, secondary and postsecondary. It is not simply that the traditional college-age group will be smaller by several million persons, with anticipated enrollment declining from 11.5 million students to 10.9 million (Joint Economic Committee, 1980). Were the rate of enrollments for the same age group increasing at 1960s levels, that drop would not occur. For numerous reasons, the concept of universal and free public education has not transcended the secondary schools, despite the hopes of some higher educators in recent decades. Not only that, but public support for free, quality public education overall is wavering. Nor has national policy warmed to the European practice of guaranteed financial support of education and training sabbaticals for adult workers (Striner, 1980).

For readers who want to pursue this discussion, contacting the authors themselves may be more helpful than a bibliography, keypieces of which are indicated in the reference sections of each chapter.

The best sources of further information are close to home. Contacting the campuses, corporations, unions, educational brokers and related groups in one's own community is the quickest way to learn about the starting points for developing real relationships among real institutions. For a brief description of organizations involved in this topic, one directory in particular may be worth consulting: *Organizations Providing Business and Economic Education Materials or Information* (Standard Oil Company, 1979).

References

Carpenter, T. *Calling the Tune: Communication Technology for Working, Learning, and Living.* Washington, D.C.: National Institute for Work and Learning, 1980.

Charner, I. *Patterns of Adult Participation in Learning Activities.* Washington, D.C.: National Institute for Work and Learning, 1980.

Fraser, B. S. *The Structure of Adult Learning, Education, and Training Opportunity in the United States.* Washington, D.C.: National Institute for Work and Learning, 1980.

Joint Economic Committee. *Human Resources and Demographics: Characteristics of People and Policy.* Washington, D.C.: Joint Economic Committee, Nov. 1980.

Lusterman, S. *Education in Industry.* New York: The Conference Board, 1977.

National Broadcasting Company. *NBC Whitepaper: If Japan Can . . . Why Can't We?* Televised June 24, 1980. New York: National Broadcasting Company, 1980.

Standard Oil Company. *Organizations Providing Business and Economic Education Materials or Information,* Chicago, Ill.: Public and Government Affairs, Standard Oil Company of Indiana, 1979.

Striner, H. E. "The Joint Role of Industry and Education in Human Resource Development." In R. Yarrington (Ed.) *Employee Training for Productivity.* Washington, D.C.: American Association of Community and Junior Colleges, 1980.

Index

Technical State University, graduate program at, 57–58

North Carolina National Bank, collaboration by, 42

North Carolina State University, cooperative research center at, 54

Northeast Illinois University, and access, 80–81

Northeastern University, and access, 80

O

O'Connor, D., 24, 26

Office of Management and Budget (OMB), 5, 8, 61

Office of Strategic Services (OSS), 35

Olson, E., 45

Omenn, G. S., 54, 55, 61, 63

Oregon, University of, Innovation Center at, 58

Organisation for Economic Co-operation and Development (OECD), 100, 108

P

Pace University, minority women at, 79

Pepsi-Cola, course evaluation for, 86

Piedmont Area Evening Degree Association (PAEDA), collaboration by, 42, 106

Piedmont Aviation, collaboration by, 42

Pinto, P. R., 40, 45

Piore, M., 101, 106, 108

Pittsburgh, University of, consulting project of, 78

Polaroid Corporation: and access, 80; and human resources management, 105; Tuition Assistance Office of, 17

Polytechnic Institute, internships at, 82

Pottinger, P. S., 6, 8

Prager, D. J., 54, 55, 61, 63

Private Industry Councils (PICs), and strategy development, 18

Project Hindsight, 48

Project Traces, 48

Q

Quality of work life, 37

R

Ravitch, D., 10, 26

RCA, skill training by, 15

Regents External Degree Program (REX), 87–88

Reid, W. J., 51, 63

Reilly, K. P., 6, 15, 85–96

Research Revitalization Act of 1980, 16

Revenue Act of 1978, Employer Educational Assistance in, 44

Ritterbush, P., 20, 26

Robock, S., 19, 26

Rockefeller, J. D., 11

Rockwell International, and graduate training, 57–58

Rogers, A., 23, 26–27

Rosow, L. A., 105, 108

Russell, L. J., 26

S

San Francisco, University of, and Asian business community, 79

Schendel, D. E., 7, 8

Schlitz Container Division, collaboration by, 42

Shadow education system, 29–46, 65

Shapero, A., 50, 63

Sherwin, E. W., 48, 63

Shore, J. E., 23, 24, 26–27, 106, 108

Singer, skill training by, 15

Skill training, premises of, 69–70

Skrovan, D. J., 37, 45

Small Business Administration, 14

Small business management training, for teaching/learning function, 14

Smith College, corporate women at, 79

Smith-Hughes Act of 1917, 34

Snow College, and access, 80

Souder, W. E., 52, 63

South Carolina, Technical Education Colleges (TEC) of, 42

Southern California, University of, community service at, 78

Southern New England Telephone Company, course evaluation for, 89

Sperry Corporation: and cooperative research, 107; course evaluation for, 87

Stack, H., 3, 8, 21, 27